the celtic story

An Official History of
Celtic Football Club

John C. Traynor

g

Grange
Lomond Books

© 1998
Published by Grange Communications Ltd
Edinburgh

Printed in the UK

ISBN 0 947782 06 0

CONTENTS

INTRODUCTION

THE CELTIC STORY is an enthralling one. It is a white-knuckle ride of emotional highs and lows, from the hardship and deprivation of Glasgow's East End in the late nineteenth century, to the comparative opulence of the spectacular new Celtic Park at the threshold of a new millennium. The 110 years in between have witnessed a succession of peaks and troughs in the fortunes of 'The People's Club' and its successive generations of faithful supporters.

In the best of times, Celtic strode the stage as European Champions, football giants on a continent previously monopolised and subsequently dominated by multi-national millionaire outfits, in stark contrast to Jock Stein's homebred squad that became immortalised as 'The Lisbon Lions'. Yet, by contrast, the same Celtic had, along the way, plumbed the very depths of mediocrity, when, faced with the humiliating prospect of unthinkable relegation, they scrambled a 3-2 victory over Dundee at Dens Park in the very last match of season 1947/48. However hard it may be to equate such wild swings in fortune, it is curiously typical of the 'fairytale' history of this most special of clubs.

Consider the magnitude of its achievements by contrast with its humble origins. Examine the nature of its unique and sometimes highly unlikely successes. Reflect on its many larger-than-life characters and their often improbable stories and you will realise that Celtic is more than just another football club. It is an institution which, despite its changing face and increasing commercialisation over the years, remains for millions across the world, an extended family and *a way of life* which enriches their very being.

Over the years, various eminent authorities have eloquently and comprehensively documented the sprawling history of Celtic, each from their own particular perspective and point in time. This is not intended as such an exercise, nor is it my objective to contest, affirm or embellish any previous version of the story. The purpose of this account is to complement earlier writings, providing an up-to-date and hopefully entertaining read for anyone so minded – to delight rather than enlighten, to edify rather than educate. The perspective is of one who cherishes all things 'Celtic': origins and traditions; fact and folklore; values, legend and legacy. If you share this perspective, you are sure to find much to savour within these pages.

In 1994, ownership and control of Celtic was wrested from the hands of the family dynasties which had shaped its destiny for 106 years, rescuing it from the very brink of bankruptcy. The nature and operation of the club was transformed almost beyond recognition in the wake of the share issue that followed. While approval of the brave new world of 'Celtic plc' is not universal, few would dispute that the club is leaner and fitter to face the challenge of the modern football *business*.

At time of writing, controversy has re-emerged over the possible future ownership of Celtic. In the midst of such speculation, everyone would do well to remember that, whoever owns the fabric of the club, its heart and soul are its supporters and its spirit will forever remain the combined birthright and legacy of those generations past, present and yet to come, without whom Celtic has little intrinsic value, anyway.

For the moment, we should simply rejoice in the rediscovered pride of the long-overdue Championship success of 1997/98.

Origins & The Maley Years
(1887 – 1940)

FOR MANY, the East End of Glasgow in 1887 was not a comfortable place. Decades before the advent of the Welfare State and its social provisions, insecure employment, poverty and hunger were daily realities for much of the population, a significant proportion of which were immigrant Irish Catholics. For these people, parish charity was central to their very existence and from such charitable roots sprang *The Celtic Football and Athletic Club.*

Inevitably, much of the burden of hardship fell on the children. To help alleviate their plight, schoolteachers and parish organisations such as the Society of St Vincent de Paul would regularly organise fundraising events for the provision of food and clothing.

Around then, increased leisure time deriving from changes in industrial working practices coincided with rapidly growing interest in organised football. The sport's mass appeal made it an obvious focus for charitable efforts and matches were often arranged to help finance parish 'Dinner Tables'.

The Irish origins of so many of Glasgow's East End parishioners gave them a particular interest in the successful exploits of the *'Edinburgh Hibernians'* club, which had emerged from a similar immigrant community in the East of Scotland and which regularly participated in such charity matches. Having carried all before them in eastern competition, Hibs became, in 1887, the first Edinburgh club to win the Scottish Cup and their enthusiastic Glasgow admirers marked the historic triumph with a celebratory reception in St Mary's Hall, the very venue which later that same year would witness the birth of Celtic.

Inspired by the stirring success of the Edinburgh Hibernians and fired by the ecstatic celebrations which followed their Scottish Cup success, East End Irish Glaswegians yearned for a football club of their own, which would provide an internal source of parish income and at the same time help establish a communal identity in their adopted homeland. So it was that a series of meetings took place, culminating in a mass assembly in the aforesaid St Mary's Hall early in November 1887. A firm decision was taken to launch the club and a committee was formed to move things along rapidly, although it would be another six months before a ball was kicked in earnest.

Prominent amongst the founding committee were the local G.P., Dr John Conway, first *Honorary President;* the forceful businessman, John Glass, a joiner to trade and original *President;* and a certain William Maley, *Match Secretary,* who was destined to go on to be Celtic's first and longest-serving manager.

But if these men and their committee colleagues were the 'workhorses' and the driving force behind the fledgling Celtic, the inspiration was the legendary *Brother Walfrid.* Born Andrew Kerins in Ballymote, County Sligo, Ireland, on 18th May, 1840 and drawn to the religious life, Walfrid's vocation took him to Glasgow, where, at the time, he was serving within the Marist teaching order as headmaster of the Sacred Heart School in the East End parish of that name. Closely associated as he was with the parish of St Mary's, from which sprang the greatest enthusiasm for setting up a community football club, his work amongst needy children and his charitable vision inevitably thrust him to the forefront of that movement.

Needless to say, in those turbulent times and within such a passionate community, the evolution of the new club was not entirely harmonious. Walfrid's strength of character and dogged determination were key factors in holding out against dissident elements to secure not only a philosophy which endures to this day in the non-sectarian policy of the club (see Appendix 1) but also one of the most evocative names in world football.

At the outset and more than once in the early years, determined efforts were made to name the new club *'Glasgow Hibernians'* rather than Walfrid's *'Celtic'*. It is easy to understand why, given the ethnic background of the community – but the visionary Walfrid understood that, though firmly rooted in, identified with and representative of an immigrant enclave, Celtic was and would increasingly grow into, a *Scottish* institution, albeit rightly proud of and cherishing its Irish heritage. The rousing name he conjured up and fought so fiercely to maintain, perfectly encapsulated the concept of a club around which he believed the kindred but religiously divided (Celtic) peoples of Ireland and Scotland could rally and unite. That name was originally pronounced *'Keltic'*, a speech mannerism Walfrid is reputed to have resolutely kept to his dying day, despite the early popular adoption of the soft pronunciation of the initial 'C', which has prevailed into modern times.

We should not be surprised at Brother Walfrid's influence over the course of Celtic's early path. Following the founder's death, William Maley, by then well established as a powerful figure in his own right, reflected in the Annual Report of June 1915 that, *"his persuasive powers, once experienced, could never be forgotten."* Certainly, Maley was eminently qualified to comment first-hand and all Celtic-minded people have cause to celebrate the legacy of a remarkable man who was arguably the greatest 'Celt' of them all.

Within a week of the historic meeting to establish the club, a tract of land was rented, on which, thanks to the sweat and toil of an army of volunteer labour, would rise the first Celtic Park. The site, adjacent to Janefield Cemetery, is nowadays the location of premises operated by the A.G. Barr soft drinks firm. A curious twist of fate, surely, as R. F. Barr of that company's forerunners was one of the earliest Celtic 'sponsors', in response to the official fundraising appeal of January 1888. It would only briefly be the club's home, however. The unreasonable demands of a rapacious landlord prompted the move in 1892 to the nearby site of today's magnificent stadium.

Celtic's First Match

Curiously, Celtic did not reserve to themselves the honour of officially opening their new ground, a task entrusted to Hibs and Cowlairs. Presumably the thinking was that maximum publicity, not to mention much-needed income, would be generated by two of the biggest names in Scottish football at the time. In the event, a 0-0 scoreline on the opening day of that year's great Glasgow Exhibition was probably something of a disappointment to the 3,000 or so festive spectators.

Twenty days later, however, on Monday 28th May, 1888, it was very different as the nation's two biggest football names of *all* time went head-to-head for the very first time in Celtic's inaugural game, a 'friendly'. Celtic had put a side together, most likely by the variety of inducements common at a time when football in Scotland was still officially amateur and players could effectively change clubs at will. It has been suggested in some quarters that this recruitment drive involved shameful underhand tactics to the severe detriment of others but such insinuations *have never been* and almost certainly *could never be* substantiated. At any rate, in the light of other allegations and relevations of the time, such detractors would do well to keep their own counsel. *"Let he who is without sin cast the first stone,"* is a quotation that comes to mind. Whatever the case may be, quality players had been attracted from many well-established outfits. Amongst them was Scottish internationalist, James Kelly, recruited from the famous Renton club. He was the father of Sir Robert ('Bob') Kelly, the resolute and sometimes crusty Chairman who would historically recall Jock Stein to Celtic Park almost eighty years later. The now-familiar and much-loved 'hoops' strip, so reminiscent of that of the 'Old Hibs' of the 1870s, would not be introduced until season 1903/04. Before then, the standard Celtic outfit was either all emerald green or vertical green and white stripes. However, on that fateful day, the following historic line-up, illustrated in the traditional 1-2-3-5 formation, turned out regaled in a specially donated original garb of white shirts, emblazoned on the right breast with a green and red Celtic cross and trimmed with a green collar:

**Dolan: Pearson, McLaughlin; W. Maley, Kelly, Murray; McCallum,
T. Maley, Madden, Dunbar & Gorevin.**

Despite Celtic's astute team-building endeavours, Rangers, who had already been in existence for going on sixteen years, were probably favourites on account of their experience as a unit. However, not untypically of what would in time come to be known as *'Old Firm'* matches, the form book went straight out the window as Celtic trumpeted their arrival with a stunning 5-2 victory.

Hail! Hail! The Celts were, emphatically, *here to stay.*

The Maley Years

So, Celtic were off and running – and what a blistering pace they began to set. That first season was characterised by the sort of free-flowing, high-scoring, attack-minded football which was to become the club's trademark. Added to the fact that they only

narrowly missed out on a major trophy, losing the Scottish Cup Final of 1889 to Third Lanark, it is not difficult to imagine the explosive impact of the newcomers – and it was no 'flash in the pan', either.

Indeed, the 'Maley Years', spanning over half a century, from 1887–1940 (during which time William Maley led Celtic, first as Match Secretary/ Player then as Secretary/Manager), covered an era which saw a constant stream of League Championships, Scottish Cups and assorted other successes.

Between the establishment of the Scottish League in 1890 and the end of the century, Celtic were Champions four times and runners-up on another three occasions, with three Scottish Cups,

William Maley

four Glasgow Cups and six Charity Cups thrown in for good measure. Not a bad start! But that's all it was – *not a bad start* – there was even better to come in the not-too-distant future.

After a bit of a stutter around the turn of the century, the show would soon be on the road again. Meanwhile, one of those great 'Milestones' in Celtic history helped to fill the void.

The Glasgow Exhibition Cup (1901 & 1902)

Eight of Scotland's top clubs contested the football tournament held to mark the Glasgow International Exhibition of 1901, in which a truly magnificent, lavishly encrusted silver trophy awaited the victors.

Already intense rivals, Celtic and Rangers confronted each other in the final. The Ibrox men carried the day in a tough, bruising and controversial encounter, with a bitter aftermath of allegation and counter allegation. That, though, was not the end of the story.

In April of the following year, Ibrox hosted a Scotland v England international at which a terracing collapse resulted in dozens of fatalities and hundreds of injuries. A massive campaign was launched in aid of the Disaster Fund, including an Anglo/Scottish competition between the respective Scottish and English league champions and runners-up. Rangers and Celtic turned out for Scotland in opposition to Sunderland and Everton. The event was talked up by the press into an unofficial British Championship and Rangers, in an excess of either gratitude or confidence, rashly put up their Glasgow Exhibition Cup as an outright prize for the winners.

Of course, the inevitable happened. Celtic saw off Sunderland, Rangers took care of Everton and the stage was set for a re-run of the previous year's showdown. Maley himself recalled the occasion in his forthright book, *'The Story of Celtic'*, as an epic double-header on 17th and 19th June, 1902. Celtic won at the second time of asking, after a 1-1 draw, with a clinching third goal in the dying moments of extra time following the 2-2 replay.

So it is that a trophy inscribed, *'Won by Rangers F.C.'* has a permanent home at Celtic Park!

Interestingly, the Disaster Fund also benefited from a Celtic/Rangers challenge match sponsored by 'Bovril' a couple of months later. This was not such a tight affair, as Celtic hammered the men from Govan 7-2 at Hampden Park on 20th August, 1902. The mighty Jimmy Quinn helped himself to one of his trademark 'hat-tricks' on a day to savour for those of a Celtic persuasion.

Within a couple of years, another 'Golden Age' beckoned. In the sixteen seasons from 1903/04–1918/19, Celtic plundered six Scottish Cups and no fewer than eleven League Championships, including six in succession from 1904/05–1909/10.

Six-In-A-Row!

Although since surpassed both by a subsequent Celtic squad and also (of recent, painful memory) by Rangers, the run of titles in the rumbustious football years between 1904 & 1910 was a staggering feat in its own right. The achievement was duly and quite rightly immortalised by Celtic's Scottish League colleagues in the form of an impressive, mounted silver shield, which to this day occupies a place of honour within the Celtic Park trophy complex. The names of the successive victorious squads are inscribed on the wreathed medallions that encircle the central Lion Rampant. This imposing relic of, at least outwardly, more gracious social times, is a fitting memorial to the talents and deeds of the great Celtic players of that era and their dominance over their contemporaries.

Representative of all who graced the colours throughout those years is this typical line-up from around the mid-point of the glory run:

Adams: McNair, Weir; Young, Loney, Hay; Bennett, McMenemy, Quinn, Somers, Hamilton.

Of the above, Adams, McNair, Loney, Hay, McMenemy and Quinn were regular first choices in all six Championship seasons. Of the others, Somers and Hamilton featured in five, Young and Bennett in four and Weir in three. Celtic's consistency at that time resulted from the Maley policy of, as far as possible, fielding the same team, week in, week out, season after season. The dramatic success of the practice was largely due to the often brilliant reliability of virtually ever-present goalkeeper, Davie Adams, the renowned half-back line of 'Sunny Jim' Young, Willie Loney and Jimmy Hay, the gifted guile of inside-right, Jimmy McMenemy ('Napoleon') and the rampaging power of legendary centre-forward, Jimmy Quinn.

Celtic lost just 23 out of 192 league games over those six seasons, amassing 305 points out of a possible 384.

Celtic Players & Officials, 1907/08, pictured with (Left to Right) Charity Cup, Scottish Cup & Glasgow Cup.
Back Row: (Left to Right) T. White, J. Kelly, T. Colgan, J. McKillop, J. Grant, M. Dunbar.
Middle Row: W. Maley (Manager), J. Young, P. Somers, J. McMenemy, D. Adams, J. Mitchell, J. Weir, R. Davis (Trainer)
Front Row: D. Hamilton, D. McLeod, W. Loney, J. Hay, J. Quinn, A. McNair.

The exhilarating winning sequence would almost certainly have been emulated by an equally great, if not greater, 'pool' over the period 1913/14-1918/19, if the bulk of the squad of 1917/18 had not been called up for War Service. Despite being so badly depleted, Celtic still managed to finish second in the league that season, just a single point behind Rangers.

So, it was only to be five out of six – but ten out of ten for effort!

The final twenty or so years of Maley's managership, while nothing like as productive as the first thirty-one (including the early years, before he was officially appointed), still yielded a further four league titles and another six Scottish Cups, as well as a clutch of the 'lesser' trophies, though at that time, the Glasgow and Charity Cups were very big events in their own right.

This particular era was arguably notable as much for the host of great Celtic players and personalities it threw up as for the ongoing haul of titles and cups. A full roll call of such 'characters' would, itself, fill a book – but three of the giants of Celtic folklore stand out from the pack: the incomparable Patsy Gallacher, the goal machine that was James Edward McGrory and the tragic *'Prince of Goalkeepers'*, John Thomson.

Patsy Gallacher

Grandfather of Scotland's 1998 World Cup frontman, Kevin Gallacher, Patsy was

Celtic Squad, 1913/14.
Back Row: (Left to Right) W. McStay, T. McGregor, J. Dodds, Jarvis.
Standing: W. Quinn (Trainer), A. McNair, W. Loney, J. Young, Davidson, J. Quinn, P. Johnstone, W. Maley (Manager).
Seated: J. Mulrooney, J. McMaster, C. Shaw, J. Cassidy, J. McMenemy.
Squatting: A. McAtee, P. Gallacher, J. Browning, A. McLean.

reputedly the most complete footballer of his time, a status which is probably the ultimate accolade, whatever the sport. In an era when fine-tuned athleticism was less important in football than it is today, the legendary inside-man had an abundance of skill, courage and imagination, allied to a natural fitness which belied his slight appearance and rather ungainly gait.

Stories abound of his playing exploits, the most enduring being that of his remarkable late equaliser against Dundee in the Scottish Cup Final of 1925, which Celtic went on to win 2-1. Patsy's meandering individual run, seemingly halted by a scything last-ditch tackle, culminated in a recovering somersault over the line with the ball wedged between his feet. The spontaneous leap was put into fresh perspective during the 1998 World Cup Finals in France, when television pundits waxed lyrical over something similar, though far less acrobatic and nowhere near as decisive, by a Mexican winger. The apparently 'gobsmacked' commentators hailed the, in truth, rather clumsy piece of ball-juggling as proof positive that the game constantly moves on - *seventy-three years after Patsy had shown how it should really be done!*

The Cup Final incident was, though, merely a particularly shining example of the outrageous array of unorthodox trickery Gallacher, an equally eccentric character off the field, regularly deployed to the ecstatic delight of fans and the utter dismay of opponents.

There will always be a place in football for genius, which cannot be suppressed – and the genius that was Patsy Gallacher would have shone through in any era.

James Edward McGrory

In the twilight of the great Patsy's days in the 'hoops', a youngster joined Celtic from his local junior club, St Roch's. A product of the rugged Garngad district of Glasgow, Jimmy McGrory was destined to follow in the footsteps of the mighty Quinn, who had not until then been convincingly replaced as spearhead of the Celtic attack (notwithstanding the heroic Joe Cassidy).

Easily the most prolific Celtic 'striker' ever, Jimmy amassed a remarkable 550 goals (still a British record) over his fifteen-year career from 1922-1937. A very high proportion of those were scored with the head, which was his awesome speciality, including the late winner in the 1925 Scottish Cup Final, rounding off Gallacher's 'wonder goal' described above.

Amongst McGrory's many prodigious scoring feats was his record haul of eight goals in the 9-0 league rout of Dunfermline at Celtic Park on 14th January, 1928.

Perhaps, though, the great man's most striking attributes were his unswerving sportsmanship and despite his greatness, genuine modesty, giving the lie to the sterile theory that good guys never win.

Jimmy went on to manage Celtic for twenty years, from 1945-1965, not the most outstandingly successful period in the club's history, perhaps – but one which nevertheless embraced a clutch of its most glorious and memorable chapters.

John Thomson

In just three full seasons between his teenage debut against Dundee on 12th February, 1927 and his shattering accidental death at the tender age of only 22, playing against Rangers at Ibrox on 5th September, 1931, 'Johnny' Thomson wrote himself into Celtic folklore as none before or since. His cat-like agility and well-documented knack of seeming to defy the laws of physics by twisting and re-launching himself in mid-air to make breathtaking saves, set him apart. Likewise, his uncanny anticipation and strength of hand and wrist, which enabled him to not only parry but *clutch* shots of awesome power.

It ranks as one of the great sporting tragedies that Celtic and Scotland were prematurely robbed of such a gifted goalkeeper, who literally 'died for the jersey' at the very height of his considerable powers.

Eulogised and lamented in verse and song, lionised by legend and immortalised in death, the haunting memory of young Thomson lingers still.

We are unlikely ever to see his like again.

Europe

"There must be some mistake, here," you're probably thinking. " Celtic never played in Europe till the early sixties. Valencia, I think it was – I was at the home game!"

Right – up to a point. In the modern era (excluding 'friendlies' and the quaint, invitational *'Friendship Cup'*, which produced a 6-3 aggregate humbling at the hands of Sedan Torchy, of France, in season 1960/61), Celtic's first appearance in recognised European competition *was* against the Spaniards. It was in the *'Fairs Cities Cup'* (the forerunner of today's UEFA Cup) of 1962/63 – I was at the game, too. In fact, John Clark's penalty miss cost me the bus sweep that night!

However, long before any of today's European cups were even thought of, the pioneering spirit with which from the outset Celtic stormed Scottish football, saw the club undertake a series of ambitious trips across Europe, carrying the football gospel to countries in which the game was just beginning to take root. As early as 1904, they became the first Scottish club to tour the continent, playing matches in the Austrian and Czech capitals, Vienna and Prague. Over the following fifty years, Celtic would go on, in a series of 'football safaris', to blaze trails to Hungary, Germany, Denmark, France and Italy, as well as visiting Switzerland to take in the 1954 World Cup Finals as a reward for the 'double' of 1953/54. In addition, they finally realised one of the earliest ambitions of the founding fathers, with trips across the Atlantic to North America in 1931 and 1951.

On one of those early continental trips, in 1914, the whimsical tale of Celtic's first 'European Cup' began to unfold. An unscheduled charity match, arranged by the Hungarian hosts without prior consultation, was played in Budapest against Burnley, who were also touring there at the time. Following an ill-tempered draw, the players refused to play extra time and as Celtic were setting off for home the next day, no replay was possible. The special trophy was withheld pending the outcome of an agreed play-off in Britain, for which Burnley gained home advantage on the toss of a coin. Celtic duly won 2-0 in England prior to season 1914/15 but never received their prize, despite forwarding the pre-arranged proportion of gate receipts to the Hungarian charity fund.

You could be forgiven for thinking that was that. However, the modern-day officials of Ferencvaros, the club that donated the original trophy, had long memories and righted the injustice almost three-quarters of a century later by flying over to present an ornate porcelain replacement 'cup' to coincide with Celtic's Centenary in 1988.

The 'Ferencvaros Vase' now occupies an honoured place in the spotlit trophy cabinet in the Celtic board room, bedecked with a plaque proclaiming it, *"to mark their first 'European Cup' victory in 1914."*

One final 'Milestone' had yet to be carved before William Maley finally moved out of the 'hot seat' into his armchair in the Celtic 'Hall of Fame', secure in the knowledge that, as long as Celtic lives on in minds and hearts, his name will be remembered.

The Empire Exhibition Trophy (1938)

Exhibitions figured prominently in the first 50 years of Celtic's history. They reached the final of the Exhibition Cup of 1888, a local competition embraced by that year's Glasgow Exhibition, losing 2-0 to Cowlairs.

The new century kicked off with the Glasgow International Exhibition of 1901. Another football tournament took place, this time national, featuring eight of Scotland's leading clubs - and another final for Celtic. Though losing again, this time to Rangers, the elaborate Glasgow Exhibition Cup was destined for a permanent home at Celtic Park as a result of the following year's events, recounted earlier.

Fifty years after the first Glasgow Exhibition and happily coinciding with Celtic's own 'Golden Jubilee', came the grand Empire Exhibition of 1938. Glasgow's contribution to the event included yet another festival of football, widened this time to include leading English clubs. All matches were played at Ibrox Stadium, a stone's throw from Bellahouston Park, where the Exhibition was centred.

Huge crowds were attracted to Celtic's ties as they progressed to their third 'exhibition' final, disposing of Sunderland (3-1 after 0-0 draw, Scorers: Divers, 2 and Crum) and Hearts (1-0, Scorer: Crum) along the way.

In the final, more difficult British opposition would have been harder to find at that time than Everton, conquerors of Rangers (2-0) and Aberdeen (3-2), who had at their disposal no fewer than ten internationalists, drawn from all four home countries. Celtic, though, were not about to stumble, as previously – *this* Exhibition Trophy (a mounted silver replica of the Exhibition Tower which was the spectacular landmark of the event) would be theirs at the first time of asking.

On Friday 10th June, 1938, a crowd of around 82,000 witnessed a wonderful final, in which the clever teamwork and telepathic forward interchanging of Celtic confronted the individual strength of Everton, powerfully led by renowned England international centre-forward, Tommy Lawton. The ninety minutes ended goalless, mainly on account of the excellent defensive display of both teams.

Early in extra time, Johnny Crum broke the deadlock, achieving the feat of scoring in each round of the competition. That was enough to secure a historic, distinctive and permanent

Empire Exhibition Trophy Team, 1938.
Back Row: (Left to Right) Geatons, Hogg, Kennaway, Morrison, Crum, Paterson.
Front Row: Delaney, MacDonald, Lyon, Divers, Murphy.

addition to the Celtic trophy collection. The team that wrote itself into the record books that day and which was decades ahead of its time tactically, was:

Kennaway: Hogg, Morrison; Geatons, Lyon, Paterson; Delaney, MacDonald, Crum, Divers & Murphy.

Sadly, when the curtain came down on William Maley's colourful and illustrious career, it was not in the most amicable of circumstances. Indeed, in the wake of a prolonged dismal spell following the Empire Exhibition success, Chairman, Tom White forced him rather grudgingly into retirement in 1940, at the age of 71.

It would be a quarter of a century before such dominance returned as Maley presided over.

'Two Jimmys': McStay & McGrory (1940 - 1965)

WORLD WAR TWO reduced Scottish football to a hotch-potch of regional leagues and localised cup competitions. The Scottish League and Scottish Cup were put into cold storage and Celtic went into hibernation. The fans, who admittedly had other things on their minds at the time, were thrust into football 'limbo' as the club, more depleted than some by service to king and country, drifted.

A Thankless Task

Former centre-half and captain, Jimmy McStay, was charged with steering Celtic through these difficult times, hampered by the awesome legacy of his predecessor and the club's apparent lack of serious competitive interest. Despite Jimmy's best endeavours, further frustrated by the board's steadfast refusal to indulge to any great extent in the wartime merry-go-round of big-name 'guest' players, Celtic's only honours over the period were the Glasgow Cup of 1940/41 and the Glasgow Charity Cup of 1942/43.

Jimmy McStay in his playing days.

Fate, then, had dealt McStay a 'dummy' hand. Compensation came, however, in the closing stages of his tenure with a quaint but enduring piece of Celtic history - a cosy 'corner' in which to enshrine the family name in the folklore of the club. Deservedly so, for the McStays have served the cause with great distinction in the persons of Jimmy himself, his brother, Willie (an earlier captain) and their descendants, latter-day Club Captain, Paul and *his* brother, also Willie. Younger brother Raymond, too, was at the club for a time.

The Victory in Europe Cup (1945)

To commemorate the cessation of hostilities and to help raise money for war charities, the Glasgow Charity Cup Committee put up a trophy intended for contention between Celtic and Rangers. The Govan club declined and it was left to Jimmy McStay's Celtic and Queen's Park to compete for outright possession of the historic silverware.

The two lined up at Hampden on 9th May, 1945 for a match which ended 1-1. In today's world of *'penalty shoot-outs'* and *'golden goals'* it is interesting to note how they (sometimes) sorted things out in those days. As a reflection of pressure, corners were taken into account and on this occasion, Celtic held the balance by three corners to two – a narrow winning margin, indeed – but enough to take the Victory in Europe Cup to Celtic Park for all time!

The triumphant Celtic team that day included two survivors from the Empire Exhibition Trophy side, Bobby Hogg and Malcolm MacDonald.

The full line-up was:

Miller: Hogg, McDonald; Lynch, Mallan, McPhail; Paton, MacDonald, Gallacher, Evans & McLaughlin.

So, the ill-fated managership of Jimmy McStay at least *ended* on a high note. His final season also saw the arrival from junior club, St Anthony's, of a young man who would develop into one of Celtic's all-time-great players, wing-half ('midfielder', in today's parlance) and centre-half, Bobby Evans.

Like Maley before him, McStay resented the way in which he was off-handedly discarded by Celtic at the finish, being left to learn of his fate from a newspaper hoarding on his way home from holiday. There is a school of thought, to which he himself probably subscribed, that he was only ever appointed, anyway, as a 'caretaker' for his successor, the club's favourite son, Jimmy McGrory - and his bitterness was open. Thankfully, though, friendship prevailed, the two former team-mates were soon reconciled and Jimmy offered his services to the new manager as a talent scout.

McGrory's Return

If Celtic were hoping for a dramatic turnaround in fortunes with the homecoming of Jimmy McGrory, they were to be sadly disappointed. His long occupancy of the manager's chair at Celtic Park brought only one solitary League Championship and two Scottish Cups - although, to be fair, he was still officially in charge for much of the landmark 1964/65 Scottish Cup success, which was the spark for so much of what followed. In addition, he was, albeit with a little 'help' from a senior colleague, the architect of three of the most celebrated and satisfying achievements in Celtic history: the 1951 St Mungo Cup, the 1953 Coronation Cup and the League Cup of 1957/58, all of which, more later. Not to forget the 'double' of 1953/54.

As a goalscorer, Jimmy had been peerless. As a competitor, he was ferocious, though scrupulously fair. As a man, he was genial, courteous, considerate and modest, almost to a fault. Paradoxically, these gentle personal characteristics, contrasting so starkly with his robust playing style, made him simultaneously the most unlikely and yet the most natural individual to be Celtic manager at that time. 'Unlikely', in that the rough and tumble of the dressing room makes no concessions to courtesy and modesty – especially when you have to deal with guys like Charlie Tully! Likewise, the cut and thrust of the football world. 'Natural', to the extent that his legendary status rendered him almost beyond reproach to the fans, while his relaxed style and accommodating nature made him the perfect foil for the real power behind the throne, Bob Kelly, who took over as Chairman from Tom White in 1947. Between them, McGrory and Kelly formed an unlikely alliance but a formidable partnership, based on tradition, high principles and an unshakeable belief in the destiny of Celtic Football Club.

It would be easy, in the light of his frequent deference to the Chairman, to dismiss McGrory as weak. But one man's deference is another's respect – and it should be remembered that the teams of that period, though short on 'bread and butter' achievement, were often highly entertaining in the traditional Celtic mould and that the underlying principles of home-breeding and youth development were to be the bedrock of spectacular future success.

Perhaps the two most notorious examples of the Chairman's will prevailing over his manager's were the transfers of Bertie Auld and Paddy Crerand. Both players, colourful, headstrong individuals who were highly skilled and great favourites with the fans, incurred Kelly's displeasure and were forced out, despite McGrory's protestations. Perhaps a stronger manager would have stood his ground on such matters, even to the extent of resignation on a point of principle. Typically, though, Jimmy accepted the setbacks, realising that they had not been inflicted lightly. Bob Kelly, for his part, was big enough to swallow his own pride and consent to the 'return of the prodigal son', with the recall of Auld early in 1965, when a need had been identified for an experienced head to marshal the young talents that were coming to fruition around then.

Thus progressed the incongruous partnership of affable manager and irascible Chairman - and thus Celtic prospered, though not always noticeably.

The first five years of the McGrory era mirrored Jimmy McStay's time exactly in terms of trophies – just one Glasgow Cup (1948/49) and one Glasgow Charity Cup (1949/50), perhaps putting his unfortunate predecessor's record into a more favourable perspective. The period also included what the third manager recalled in his book, 'A Lifetime in Paradise', as, "… the worst experience I've ever had in football; the spectre of relegation haunting Celtic."

It was the last game of season 1947/48 and if Celtic had lost, depending on results elsewhere, they could have been relegated for the first and only time. The very thought sent shivers of trepidation and revulsion through the great man and the manner in which the day unfolded must have been agonising for everyone involved.

The first half saw an incredible *three* Celtic goals disallowed (McPhail, 2 and Lavery) before recent signing, Jock Weir, squeezed one home following a goalmouth melee – only for Dundee to equalise just before the interval. On the hour mark, things got desperate as Dundee took the lead and the Second Division (Division 'B' as it was then known) loomed large. A characteristic Celtic onslaught seemed doomed to failure before Weir ended the agony with a scrambled late 'one-two', the crucial winner coming just two minutes from time. A 'hat-trick' in such stressful circumstances surely qualifies Jock Weir as one of Celtic's most inspired signings ever and a 'snip' at £7,000 from Blackburn Rovers.

Getting back to comparative five-year records, McStay had actually gone one trophy better in *his* stint, with the one-off Victory in Europe success. It wouldn't be too long, though, before McGrory drew level and indeed, pulled ahead in the 'special event' stakes, as Celtic embarked on a brief burst of distinctive achievement between 1951 and 1954.

Before that, however, the Scottish Cup finally made its long-overdue return to Celtic Park at the end of season 1950/51, ending a horrendous thirteen-year major trophy famine since the League Championship success of 1937/38. A first-half John McPhail goal against Motherwell in the final was enough to secure a sixteenth cup win and clear Celtic to pack the old trophy for the imminent voyage to the United States and Canada, just as they had done twenty years earlier following victory over the same opposition.

The tour was a rollicking success, both in the playing sense and socially, as Celtic received a rapturous reception from their fanatical North American public. The only sour note sounded, was during and after the 3-1 win over German fellow-tourers, Eintracht Frankfurt, in New York. Enraged at decisive penalty awards against them and the ensuing defeat, German players and spectators reacted violently. On-field trouble flared and fists flew, engulfing even the local pipe band, led by a Scot named McGonagle. In the aftermath and for no apparent reason, the blameless Jimmy McGrory took one on the chin as the players left the field at time-up.

The party returned to Scotland in late June to prepare for the new season – and there was some other important business to attend to, as well!

The St Mungo Cup (1951)

Glasgow Corporation and the S.F.A. collaborated in staging the St Mungo Cup as part of the Festival of Britain celebrations, involving all sixteen First Division clubs. On the basis that a festival is an exhibition of sorts and given Celtic's track record in previous 'exhibition' football, it was always a fair bet that they might do rather well in the competition – and so it proved, despite a miserable seventh-place finish in the preceding league season.

Celtic came through against Hearts, Clyde (despite twice falling two goals behind the 'Bully Wee') and Raith Rovers to confront a powerful Aberdeen side in the final on Wednesday, 1st August, 1951, before a crowd of over 80,000. It wasn't shaping up like the Celts' day as, in not much more than half-an-hour, they fell two behind for the third time in the competition, albeit against the run of play.

The first reverse came after twenty minutes when goalkeeper, George Hunter, failed to clear a back-header by Aberdeen centre-forward, Hamilton and Yorston forced the ball home at the post. Hunter suffered a head injury in this action and had to leave the field for treatment, being temporarily replaced between the sticks by right-half, Bobby Evans. The unfortunate goalie returned, patched up, just in time to concede a second in the thirty-fourth minute, as right-winger, Bogan, an ex-Celt, exploded a shot behind him from 18 yards.

The omens were not good. Then the enigmatic Charles Patrick Tully helped turn the game around with a typical piece of his impertinent gamesmanship, bouncing a corner-post throw-in off an Aberdeen defender for a corner, which he himself slung into the box for Sean Fallon to shoot home through a ruck of players. Five minutes to half time and Celtic were back in it, poised for a characteristic second-half surge towards victory. Doubt would now be creeping into Aberdeen heads, well aware as they were of Celtic's never-say-die cup-fighting tradition and superiority on the day, notwithstanding the scoreline as they trooped off at the interval.

Sure enough, four minutes into the second period, Fallon struck again to equalise, having been sent clear by inside-right, Walsh, to beat 'keeper, Martin, all ends up. As Celtic sustained the pressure, Walsh himself delivered the *coup de grâce* twenty minutes from time, sweeping home a Tully cross following one of the Irishman's trademark dribbles, which was shrouded in controversy. Aberdeen hotly protested that the ball had crossed the by-line before being centred. It has to be said, though, that legendary Scottish referee, Jack Mowat, was well up with play and saw no infringement. The disputed winner meant that Walsh had scored in every round, emulating John Crum's feat in the Empire Exhibition Trophy thirteen years earlier.

Contentious as the decisive strike may have been, though, the controversy was nothing compared to the row which followed Celtic's discovery that the curiously ornate cup, adorned with fish, mermaids, life belts and longboats, of all things, was a recycled yachting trophy, dating back to 1894. It had been refurbished to serve as the object of a rather less glamorous football match in 1912 between Provan Gasworks and Glasgow Police. The distinct whiff of parsimony surrounding the cup mushroomed to a billowing stench when it transpired that the city fathers had had the audacity to foist their 'changeling' onto the St Mungo competition, suitably re-dedicated. Celtic, understandably (if somewhat theatrically) outraged, went so far as to offer to pay for an appropriate replacement–but the storm eventually blew over unresolved and the third-hand St Mungo Cup duly took its allotted place amongst the club's memorabilia.

In retrospect and on the basis that the winning, itself, is more important than the pedigree of any trophy, it is probably a blessing that the substitution never took place. If

Jimmy McGrory with the League Cup, which Celtic won
twice under him, in 1956 and 1957.

it had, Celtic would have been deprived of what is arguably its most distinctive artefact and certainly one of its most intriguing stories.

The victorious St Mungo Cup heroes were:

Hunter: Haughney, Rollo; Evans, Mallan, Baillie; Collins, Walsh, Fallon, Peacock & Tully.

Six of this team (the fullback partnership of Haughney and Rollo, wing-half, Evans and forwards, Collins, Walsh and Peacock) would appear in the same positions two years later in the final match of the Coronation Cup. Charlie Tully would have made it a 'magnificent seven' but for injury ruling him out of that final.

Despite the St Mungo boost and the understandable optimism it generated, the ensuing two seasons were ones of potential unfulfilled, with the Glasgow Charity Cup of 1952/53 the only crumb of comfort. Thus was the pattern established for the frustrating fifties, which had opened so brightly but throughout which, inconsistency blighted the club and good teams of great players like Evans, Peacock, Collins, Fernie, McPhail, Mochan and Tully delivered only a handful of major trophies. However, as we shall hear, they included some of the most memorable days and at least one of the sweetest results in Celtic history.

The Flag

Before the good days returned, club and supporters had to endure one of their blackest episodes, which brought Celtic to the very edge of oblivion. Present-day fans who shuddered at the prospect of being closed down in the days leading up to the 1994 takeover will understand the extreme anxiety experienced, though the circumstances were very different.

Following crowd trouble during and after the Celtic v Rangers match at Celtic Park on New Year's Day, 1952, the S.F.A. ordered Celtic, amongst other measures, to remove the Irish flag which always flew on match days in recognition of the club's origins. The dubious justification for the order was that the flying of the tricolour was, somehow, in itself, an act of provocation and an incitement to disorderly conduct. As well as being a rather perverse piece of logic, the order was, in fact, outwith the Association's powers and Chairman, Bob Kelly, decided to challenge the slur on Celtic's good name, confront the underlying malice and repel the blatant attack on the club's fundamental right to *be* Scottish, while respectfully honouring Irish roots. Under threat of expulsion, Kelly resolved to stand his ground fearlessly, even to the point of disbanding football operations altogether, effectively closing the doors.

Serious stuff! In the end, though, sanity prevailed and the tawdry affair fizzled out, more through a growing realisation of its danger to collective self-interest than any goodwill towards Celtic. It must be pointed out, however, that when the storm clouds were gathering, strong and welcome support for Celtic's stand against the forces of darkness within the Scottish football hierarchy came from none other than Rangers Football Club. The S.F.A.'s self-inflicted dilemma was rather tortuously resolved by having the contentious ruling diluted, deferred and in the end, discreetly reversed. The flag did come down for a time but only during the summer shut-down, reappearing at the start of season 1952/53, as usual – and so ended an unsavoury attempt at ritual humiliation under the cunning guise of public order interest. Imagine the discomfiture of its architects over the irony of Celtic's next 'Milestone' a year or so down the line, of which, more shortly.

Not long before the 'flag' fiasco, late in 1951, the need for cover in the centre of defence coincided with a dearth of leadership and guidance for the promising but young and inexperienced side of the day. McGrory and Kelly began to wrestle with the idea of appointing a player-coach but could not settle on a suitable candidate. Chief scout, Jimmy Gribben, was roped into the discussions and he came up with a startling proposal to pluck a virtual unknown from the obscurity of Welsh non-league football. Jimmy McGrory had only a vague recollection of the man from his days with Albion Rovers but Gribben convinced his bosses to back his judgement. Though his signing caused a lot of head scratching amongst commentators and supporters, the impact of Jock Stein was to be both immediate and further-reaching than anyone could possibly have dreamt at the time.

Despite the newcomer's undoubted steadying and inspiring influence, season 1952/53 was distinguished only by the capture of the Charity Cup and that, somewhat fortunately, after surviving a poor semi-final display against Third Lanark on the toss of a coin. A highly entertaining side-show came, however, in a celebrated feat of Charlie Tully's in the Scottish Cup third round versus Falkirk at Brockville. Turning 2-0 down, Celtic seemed to have grabbed themselves a lifeline when Charlie 'scored' direct from a curling corner early in the second half, only to suffer the anguish of being ordered to retake the kick. The referee had spotted some infringement, most likely the ball being illegally placed outwith the corner segment, a ploy well within Tully's repertoire, it has to be admitted. Undaunted, the bold 'Bhoyo' promptly produced a carbon copy of the original delivery and the ball looped straight into the Falkirk net a second time. In case anyone chooses to dismiss this as a fluke, it should be remembered that Charlie had done exactly the same thing a few weeks previously in a Northern Ireland v England international. The terracing erupted, crush barriers gave way and amid further such mayhem, Celtic inevitably went on to recover and win, with further strikes from Fernie and (John) McGrory. That was that, though, as far as the Scottish Cup was concerned. The Charity Cup brought a measure of consolation, with a 3-1 victory over Queen's

Celtic Team 1950

Park in a final which featured a debut 'double' from new, hard-hitting centre-forward, Neil Mochan, an £8,000 signing from Middlesbrough.

The season had started badly, blighted by the long absence of Bobby Collins as the result of a nasty broken arm, sustained during an April tour of Ireland, which kept him sidelined until December. It ended likewise, with the team trailing in eighth in the league, an improvement, nonetheless, of one place on the previous season's finish – but this continuing dismal form was about to be utterly confounded by remarkable 'close-season' events.

The Coronation Cup (1953)

A collaborative venture of the respective Scottish and English Football Associations and Leagues, the Coronation Cup brought together the then elite of British football .... and Celtic! This is not a sleight on the club, simply an honest appraisal of its relative standing at the time. The full line-up was: Arsenal, Manchester United, Tottenham Hotspur, Newcastle United, Rangers, Hibernian, Aberdeen and Celtic.

Of the English contingent, Arsenal were reigning League Champions, while Man. United and Spurs were their immediate two predecessors. Newcastle had won the F.A. Cup in 1951 and 1952. From a Scottish perspective, Rangers and Hibs had been the dominant forces north of the border since the end of the war, having shared the previous seven League Championships and Aberdeen had run Rangers close in the recent Scottish Cup Final, taking them to a replay.

Apart from crowd-pulling potential, reputation and a certain tendency to excel in events of this kind, Celtic had precious little claim to a place in such exalted company and their inclusion was openly criticised in circles hostile to the club. Such bile, of course, only served to make the subsequent turn of events all the sweeter. Particularly coming so soon after the unseemly outcry over the Irish flag, which, by implication, called into question the extent of Celtic's commitment to its Scottish (and by extension, British) nationality.

Happily, common sense and commercial interest prevailed, just as it had done the previous year and the highly unlikely events of that summer would weave their way into Celtic folklore, memorably recorded for posterity in the amusing lyrics of one of the supporters' more imaginative anthems.

The first round paired Celtic with Arsenal. The mighty 'Gunners' seemed to think they were onto something of a 'walkover' and weren't shy about making that opinion public. How their arrogance rebounded on them, as Celtic struck irresistible form and humiliated the English champions by a 1-0 scoreline which in no way reflected their superiority on the day.

When Manchester United, first-round conquerors of Rangers, were disposed of 2-1 in the second round, the smirks were wiped off the faces of Celtic's earlier detractors. The prospect of a Coronation Cup showdown between, of all possible permutations, Celtic and Hibs (who had, less unexpectedly, overcome Spurs and Newcastle in the other half of the draw), was no laughing matter.

The final which few, if any, would have predicted took place at Hampden Park on the evening of Wednesday 30th May, 1953, spawning that immortal line from the 'Coronation Cup Song':

"... and oh, what a scene – the terracings were covered in banners of green!"

According to James E. Handley in his meticulous book, *'The Celtic Story'*, the match was played out at an exhilarating pace, on a still, pleasant, windless night and on a surface which, after the rain, was smooth and easy. Celtic took the lead around the half-hour mark. The gifted Willie Fernie, deputising for the injured Charlie Tully (this was the only personnel or positional change made by Celtic throughout the competition), set up the spectacular opener. Latching onto a Jock Stein clearance, he flicked the ball into the path of Neil Mochan, who almost burst the net with a first-time, thirty-yard rocket. The shot came at goalkeeper, Tommy Younger, out of a setting sun and he probably never even saw it!

Thereafter, despite Hibs' best endeavours, spearheaded by their 'Famous Five' forward line, Celtic held firm. Jock Stein and Bobby Evans marshalled the defence brilliantly, bolstered by the inspired performance of goalkeeper, Johnny Bonnar, who made this his finest hour.

The match was clinched three minutes from time, inside-right, Walsh, netting the decisive strike following an incisive move sparked by a typical Evans interception and pass.

The following great team had written a particularly glorious chapter in the magical history of the Celtic Football Club:

Bonnar: Haughney, Rollo; Evans, Stein, McPhail; Collins, Walsh, Mochan, Peacock & Fernie.

The Stein dividend carried over into season 1953/54, which, in spite of a depressingly characteristic slow start, produced Celtic's first 'double' for forty years. After failing to even qualify from their League Cup section and losing out to Rangers in a Glasgow Cup semi-final replay, a masterly positional switch took Neil Mochan from his central attacking role to a roving left-wing beat and brought devastating results. 'Neilly' banged in twenty-six goals from his wide berth and the team clicked in the league, finishing five points clear of runners-up, Hearts.

Scottish Cup, 1954

Starting with a first round 'bye', the Scottish Cup entailed three close-fought 'away' ties against Falkirk (2-1), Stirling Albion (4-3) and Hamilton Academicals (2-1) en route to a semi-final confrontation with old cup rivals, Motherwell. Hampden Park housed 102,000 spectators for a 2-2 draw before Celtic came out on top, 3-1, in front of an incredible mid-week crowd of 93,000.

In the final on 24th April, 1954, strong opposition was anticipated by an Aberdeen who had thrashed Rangers 6-0 (*yes, 6-0*) in the 'semi' – and they were not to disappoint. The 'Dons' would go on to win the league the following year but *this* was destined to be Celtic's day, as a fairly evenly divided crowd of almost 130,000 partisan souls packed Hampden to bursting point.

A tight first half ended with the combatants still locked together at 0-0 but the goal action was not long delayed after the restart. Celtic broke the deadlock when a speculative Mochan 'special' was deflected into goal by the unfortunate Aberdeen 'pivot', Young, five minutes into the second half. There was scarcely time for the celebrations to subside before the equaliser. Aberdeen centre-forward, Buckley, outpaced Stein, whose 'minder', Bobby Evans, was, for once, not in position to mop up and Bonnar was left without a prayer. It was all up for grabs again and with twenty-five minutes remaining, Willie Fernie drew the Aberdeen defence with one of his mesmerising dribbles to set the winner on a plate for Sean Fallon.

The action continued fast and furious through to time-up but Celtic had done enough to ensure that the Scottish Cup would join the League Championship trophy on the Celtic Park sideboard – and half of Glasgow gave thanks.

Seven of the Coronation Cup heroes also lined up that day in the following team:

Bonnar: Haughney, Meechan; Evans, Stein, Peacock; Higgins, Fernie, Fallon, Tully & Mochan.

As reward for the wonderful achievements of the preceding twelve months, the club took the players to the World Cup Finals in Switzerland that summer. With the great gift of hindsight, it is not difficult to suggest that the trip may have influenced the future career of Jock Stein rather more than most.

On their return, contrary to understandably heightened expectations, the old frailties had resurfaced by the time the new season got underway and the next couple of years were ones of unremitting frustration. Stein picked up an ankle injury that finished his playing career and he began to concentrate on coaching duties. Many of the other stalwarts also disappeared for one reason or another and it was season 1956/57 before another major victory, when Bobby Evans lofted the League Cup after Celtic's first success in the competition at the *eleventh* attempt, beating Partick Thistle 3-0 in the replay of a goalless draw.

Welcome though that overdue win was, it was the final of the same competition the following year that produced the result of the decade and arguably the single most celebrated scoreline in Celtic history, on which Jimmy McGrory must have dined a thousand times. Well, if he didn't, he ought to have!

Coinciding with my own flowering awareness of the football scene (my earliest recollections being the disappointment of Scottish Cup Final defeats by Clyde and Hearts in 1955 and 1956 respectively), I knew in my young heart that there was something *special* about Celtic. That mine really *was* the best team in the world – despite the glaring lack of proof.

And then it happened …

Celtic 7, Rangers 1

This was the day when simply everything went right for Celtic and the tantalising fifties potential was richly fulfilled in ninety minutes of joyous domination of their greatest tormentors. Rangers had been League Champions for the previous two seasons and took the field on 19th October, 1957 as red-hot favourites.

From the outset, though, the Ibrox rearguard was overwhelmed and the wonder is that their goal remained intact for so long against the opening onslaught. Celtic's classy halfback trio of Fernie, Evans and Peacock shackled the midfield, allowing the forwards to swarm all over a beleaguered Rangers defence.

The inevitable breakthrough came in twenty minutes from a Sammy Wilson volley and the flood tide continued. Bobby Collins almost broke the crossbar with a long-range

Billy McPhail heads home Celtic's third.

'pile-driver'. Charlie Tully clipped the post from an acute angle–but despite such close calls, the floodgates held until Neil Mochan, whose pace and power had been a constant menace down the left, grabbed a second just before the interval.

With the wind and sun at their backs going into the second half, Rangers probably thought they had weathered the storm and could set about turning things around. How wrong can you be? Those Ibrox unfortunates were about to find out, as the procession continued unabated towards their greatest-ever humiliation in a record result for a Scottish national cup final.

A further five Celtic goals brought just a solitary reply. The second-half damage took the form of a 'hat-trick' from Billy McPhail, a second strike from Mochan and a late penalty from Willie Fernie. Long before the final whistle, blind panic had set in amongst the blue jerseys and the bedraggled 'Gers must have been praying for an end to the mauling.

On that never-to-be-forgotten autumn afternoon, Celtic sent out:

Beattie: Donnelly, Fallon; Fernie, Evans, Peacock; Tully, Collins, McPhail, Wilson & Mochan.

The '7-1' scoreline was instantaneously chiselled into Celtic folklore and the reputedly lucky number, *'Se-ven'*, was enthusiastically adopted as a terracing mantra for many years to come on Glasgow 'derby' days.

In the warm afterglow of such a gala performance, anything seemed possible – but

Willie Fernie makes it seven from the penalty spot.

it was a seductive illusion. By a cruel twist of fate, Jimmy McGrory's most spectacular managerial result was also his 'major' swansong. Though he would occupy the manager's chair for another seven-and-a-half years, he would never again lead the club to top-level success. They were to be further 'wilderness years', such as Celtic supporters have, across the decades, learnt to endure with fortitude. However, in the midst of mediocrity, there would come a dazzling ray of hope.

A Glimpse of the Future

With domestic honours limited in the late fifties and early sixties to a smattering of Glasgow and Charity Cups, the startling charge of the emerging young Celts of 1963/64 to the semi-final of the European Cup Winners' Cup simultaneously heralded an imminent 'New Dawn' and highlighted the need for shrewder guidance. Celtic only qualified for the event by dint of disastrously losing the 1963 Scottish Cup Final to Rangers, who, as League Champions, had already secured a place in the European Cup. The cavalier, attacking style of the youthful side produced impressive aggregate victories over Basle of Switzerland (10-1), Yugoslavs, Dinamo Zagreb (4-2) and Czechoslovakia's Slovan Bratislava (2-0) before coming up against the tough Hungarians of MTK Budapest.

The 3-0 first-leg win at Celtic Park on a sunny April evening in 1964 could have been even more emphatic but should, in any case, have been enough to ensure a place in the final. Sadly, though, youthful and tactical naivety was heavily punished in a bruising 'away' leg, which was lost 4-0. There was much dark muttering about the referee (who turned a blind eye to much 'Magyar' mayhem and certainly seemed a trifle too cosy amongst the MTK party at the after-match banquet); but when all was said and done, Celtic's narrow failure to go all the way in their first foray in the tournament was mainly due to a lack of seasoned managerial professionalism.

This is not intended as outright criticism of Jimmy McGrory. His plans were persistently undermined by the intrusion into football matters of his well-meaning but overbearing and sometimes misguided Chairman, for whom the genial, pipe-smoking manager had, perhaps, a trifle too *much* respect for his own and the club's good. Somehow, though, the collective efforts of these two opposites took Celtic, often stumbling, to the verge of greatness and throughout the lean years, better things were bubbling under.

The traditional Celtic youth policy was clearly beginning to bear fruit – and the 'Second Coming' of Jock Stein was on the horizon.

'The Big Man': The Stein Era (1965 – 1978)

Jock Stein

THE TWELVE-AND-A-BIT SEASONS of Jock Stein's managership (he arrived at the tail-end of 1964/65 and missed the entire 1975/76 term as a result of serious injuries suffered in a car crash in the summer of 1975) were unparalleled in terms of sustained competitive success. Not since the first half of the Maley years had the major national trophies been plundered so regularly and never in such an unbroken sequence, epitomised by the *original* 'Nine-in-a-Row' (1965/66-1973/74).

His unhappy final season of 1977/78, undermined from the outset by the devastating 'close-season' departure to Liverpool of Kenny Dalglish and further destabilised by the loss through major injury of key players, Pat Stanton and Danny McGrain, was barren. That apart, though, Jock brought either the League Championship or the Scottish Cup, or both, to Celtic Park every year he was in charge. In four of those seasons, his teams did the 'double' of both premier competitions and in two others, the 'treble', by the addition of the third of the big three, the League Cup. This, the youngest of Scottish football's major events, inaugurated in season 1946/47 following the success of a similar competition during the Second World War years, was captured six times in all under Stein and five times in succession from 1965 to 1969 inclusive. Had it not been for a dramatic and perplexing reversal of League Cup trends, however, Celtic's domestic record would have been even more sensational under

picture gallery

tropHíes

European Cup
Lisbon, 25th May, 1967.
Celtic 2 Inter Milan 1
(Scorers: Gemmell, Chalmers)

Glasgow Cup
(Won by Celtic 29 times)
See 'Celtic Honours'

Victory in Europe Cup
Hampden, 9th May, 1945.
Celtic 1 Queen's park 1
(Celtic won by 3 corners to 2)

Glasgow Exhibition Cup
17th & 19th June, 1902.
Celtic 3 Rangers 2
(a.e.t., 2-2 after 90 minutes)

Scottish League Shield
(Commemorates Celtic's
'Six-in-a-Row' League
Championships,
1904/1905-1909/10.)

St. Mungo Cup
Hampden, 1st August, 1951.
Celtic 3 Aberdeen 2
(Scorers: Fallon 2, Walsh)

Detail from Board Room trophy cabinet..
The intriguing 'Ferencvaros Vase' (See 'Maley Years'–Europe) is second from right in bottom row.

Empire Exhibition Trophy
Ibrox, 10th June, 1938.
Celtic 1 Everton 0
(a.e.t. Scorer: Crum)

Coronation Cup
Hampden, 30th May, 1953.
Celtic 2 Hibernian 0
(Scorers: Mochan, Walsh)

Lisbon Lions

The 'Lisbon Lions' were, arguably, Celtic's greatest ever side.

Back Row (Left to Right): Jim Craig, Tommy Gemmell, Billy McNeill (Captain), Manager Jock Stein, Ronnie Simpson, Bobby Murdoch, John Clark.

Front Row: Jimmy Johnstone, Willie Wallace, Steve Chalmers, Bertie Auld, Bobby Lennox.

The Lions display the European Cup to the fans during the ecstatic 'Gala Night' celebrations at Celtic Park on their return from Lisbon, 26th May, 1967,

Jock Stein and the European Cup are shepherded through the joyous throng by a posse of 'Glasgow's finest'.

'The Big Man' finds the big Cup a bit of a handful.

Legends

Three giants of Scottish football. Jock Stein, Billy McNeill and Bill Shankly, pictured together at McNeill's testimonial dinner in 1975. Shankly declared Stein 'immortal' after the Lisbon triumph.

Two great Scottish captains. Billy McNeill and Billy Bremner lead their men out for the second leg of the titanic European Cup semi final of 1970. Celtic won 2-1 on the night at Hampden and 3-1 on aggregate following the great 1-0 victory at Elland Road, Leeds, in the first leg. It had been dubbed 'The Final before the Final' but turned out to be no more than the prelude to the nightmare of Milan.

Roy Aitken was a long-term, faithful Celtic servant. He scored in the 4-2 1978/79 title-clinching win over Rangers and amongst many other achievements, skippered Celtic to the Centenary 'double'.

Bobby Collins was the 'Pocket Dynamo' of Celtic's fifties squads before moving to an influential role with Leeds United.
He played in the St. Mungo and Coronation Cup winning sides and the '7-1' League Cup Final v Rangers.

Bobby Evans, seen here raising the League Cup after the 1956, 3-0 victory over Partick Thistle (Celtic's first win in the tournament at the eleventh attempt), was one of the finest players ever to don the 'hoops'. After joining Celtic from junior club, St. Anthony's, in the forties, Bobby won his first major award in the 1951 Scottish Cup victory over Motherwell. He went on to captain the victorious St. Mungo Cup side and starred in the historic 1953 Coronation Cup win.

A truly great 'wing-half' (midfielder), Bobby was a stalwart of the 1953/54 'double' winning squad and also savoured the supreme delight of the '7-1' game before his departure to Chelsea.

Following in the proud family tradition, Paul McStay played with great distinction in successful Celtic sides before assuming the captaincy in the difficult nineties. He tasted success in that role, at last, with the 1995 Scottish Cup win.

Two awesome sixties 'strikers', Joe McBride (left) and Willie Wallace.

Left to Right: Manager McGrory, Sean Fallon, Billy McPhail, trainer Johnstone and Bobby Evans admire
Bertie Peacock's 1957 League Cup medal.

centenary

Manager Billy McNeill and his squad line up behind their Centenary haul of silverware, the Scottish Cup (left), the Centenary Cup (centre) and the League Championship Trophy.

The Centenary Cup was won on 7th August; 1988,in a special commemorative match against the colourful Brazilians of Cruzeiro Belo Horizonte. Celtic won 4-2, courtesy of a typical Frank McAvennie strike and an Andy Walker 'hat-trick'.

Back Row (Left to Right): M. McGhee, W. Stark, L. Baillie, M. McCarthy, A. Rogan, D. Whyte.

Middle Row: B. Scott (Physio), M. Smith, T. Burns, A. Rough, P. Bonner, I. Andrews, F. McAvennie, O. Archdeacon, T. Craig, (Asst. Manager)

Front Row: J. MIller, P. Grant, R. Aitken, Billy McNeill, P. McStay, C. Morris, A. Walker.

Frank McAvennie's two late goals in the 1988 Scottish Cup Final clinched the Centenary 'double'.

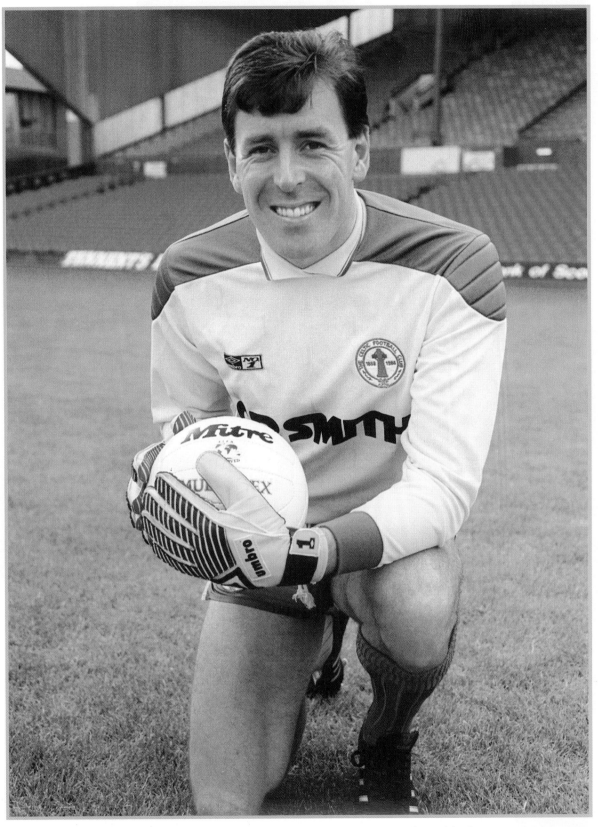

Celtic and Republic of Ireland goalkeeper, Pat ('Packie') Bonner, was a stalwart of the Centenary
squad of 1987/88.

scottish cup '95

Manager Tommy Burns and his squad pictured with the Scottish Cup.

Back Row (Left to Right): W. Falconer, A. Mowbray, P. Bonner, G. Marshall, S. Gray, P. O'Donnell.

Middle Row: B. Scott (Physio), P. Grant, T. McKinlay, T. Boyd, P. van Hooijdonk, M. Mackay, M. McNally, R. Vata, W. Stark (Asst. Manager).

Front Row: A. Walker, S. Donnelly, P. McStay (Captain), T. Burns, A. Thom, B. McLaughlin, J. Collins.

Pierre van Hooijdonk heads the ninth-minute winner at Hampden.

Tommy Burns and Billy Stark with the Scottish Cup.

The Sponsor's hoarding tells the story of this joyous picture.

Captain, Paul McStay and scorer van Hooijdonk show off the trophy.

grand old memories

Celtic F.C. 1955

Back Row (Left to Right): M. Haughney, S. Fallon, J. Bonnar, R. Evans, J. Stein, B. Peacock.

Front Row: R. Collins, W. Fernie, J. Walsh, C. Tully, N. Mochan.

Celtic v Aberdeen, Scottish Cup Final 1937. Celtic won 2-1, with goals from Johnny Crum and Willie Buchan.

New European Champions, Celtic, defeated the reigning World Club Champions, Penarol of Uruguay, 2-1 in a 'friendly'
at Celtic Park in September, 1967, with a 'double' from Willie Wallace.

Jimmy Johnstone, pictured above, destroyed Red Star Belgrade almost single-handedly in the European Cup of 1968/69 at Celtic Park.

Celtic won 5-1 with 'Jinky' scoring twice and laying on two others in a devastating second half. Steve Chalmers acclaims one of the goals.

Celtic lost narrowly to Liverpool in the semi final of the European Cup Winners' Cup of 1965/66, as a result of a refereeing blunder at Anfield. The above action is from the first leg, at Hampden.

Leeds United 'keeper Gary Sprake, can do nothing about Bobby Murdoch's drive for Celtic's second in the 2-1 Hampden win in the 1970 European Cup semi final.

Mighty John Hughes, scorer of the first Celtic goal, leads the lap of honour after the 1970 European Cup semi final victory.

Tommy Gemmell's thunderous drive gives Celtic an unlikely lead in the ill-fated 1970 European Cup Final v Feyenoord.

Willie Wallace and Wim Jansen in the Celtic v
Feyenoord 1970 European Cup Final.

Jimmy Johnstone weaves his magic.

Paul Wilson heads his own and Celtic's second in the 3-1 victory over Airdrie in the 1975 Scottish Cup Final.

A jubilant Celtic squad celebrate the historic 2-1 Centenary Cup Final victory over Dundee United, 1988.

A flashing 'Dixie' Deans header for the first of his 'hat-trick' in the 1972 Scottish Cup Final win (6-1) v Hibs.

The victorious Celtic squad with the League Cup after the 1966, 1-0, victory over Rangers.

Bobby Lennox slots home goal number two in the 4-0 demolition of Rangers in the 1969 Scottish Cup Final.

championship squad '97/'98

Pre-season line-up for 1997/98 Championship season.
(Key players, Jonathan Gould, Marc Rieper and Paul Lambert, joined during the season).
Back Row: (Left to Right): P. Grant, C. Hay, T. Johnson, G. Marshall, S. Kerr, S. Donnelly, D. Hannah, H. Larsson.
Middle Row: B. Scott (Physio), S. Gray, A. Stubbs, E. Annoni, M. Mackay, M. Wieghorst, C. Burley, T. Boyd, M. MacLeod(Asst. Coach).
Front Row: D. Jackson, B. McLaughlin, M. Burchill, J. McNamara, W. Jansen (Head Coach), T. McKinlay, A. Thom, S. Mahe, P. O'Donnell.

Simon Donnelly

Henrik Larsson

Jackie McNamara

Morten Wieghorst

picture gallery

Big Jock. For they reached the final an astonishing *thirteen years in a row* from 1965/66-1977/78 (his first and last terms respectively), winning only one of the last eight. That merciful victory in 1974, was special, in more ways than one. Firstly, because it broke up what would have been an embarrassing run of eight successive final defeats (it was bad enough, as it was, for heaven's sake) and secondly, because of the result (Celtic 6, Hibernian 3) and the exhilarating performance.

In all, two or more of Scotland's three major trophies came to Celtic Park in ten of Stein's twelve full seasons at the helm, including the first seven in succession. Only in one season out of his first ten (1972/73) did the club and its fans have to settle for a single 'major' and even that year, it was the best of them all, the League Championship. His parting shot was the 'double' of 1976/77 before the inevitable, sad decline of that ill-fated final season.

With such a formidable domestic record, allied to the club's high European standing over the period, following the phenomenal feat of winning the European Champions' Cup at the first attempt in 1967, it is difficult to dispute the 'Stein Era' as the zenith of Celtic's achievements to date. Never before or since were such pinnacles scaled, as Stein's 'Green Machine' hoisted the reputation of Scottish club football to an all-time high.

As one privileged to experience first-hand the heady success of that glorious epoch, I can say, without much fear of contradiction, that those really *were* the days.

The Making of a Legend

Jock Stein's playing record prior to joining Celtic was the very essence of mediocrity. His junior days with Blantyre Victoria were followed by a spell at Albion Rovers before disappearing into the wilderness of Welsh non-league football with Llanelli. All that time he was no more than an honest-to-goodness jobbing centre-half, hardened and focused by his earlier working life in the bowels of the earth as a miner.

Fortunately for Stein himself and everyone else connected with Celtic, when Jimmy Gribben suggested him for that player/coach vacancy towards the end of 1951, Bob Kelly seemed to remember him rather better than Jimmy McGrory did, recalling something in his play that suggested leadership potential. Whether real or imagined, that happy recollection resulted in the arrival at Celtic Park of arguably the biggest single football influence in the club's history.

Perhaps through an awareness of his own limitations, Jock had always been something of a student of the game, forever seeking to maximise such talent as he had. That ability to channel, firstly his own, then others' efforts into *what they could do well,* was the key to his genius. Combined with uncanny motivational skills and an instinctive individual understanding of how to handle different personalities, his knack of bringing out the best in people could *and did* turn good players into great ones and made the already great, magnificent. It was an irresistible formula that would, in time, propel Celtic to unparalleled heights and repay the club a thousandfold for the faith invested in him at a low point in his career.

The Stein influence was first brought to bear as player and captain when he found himself promoted rather unexpectedly to the first team due to the loss of form and injury of first-choice centre-halves, Alex Boden and Jimmy Mallan. Jock quickly made himself indispensable and went on to lead the team to glory in the Coronation Cup and the 1953/54 'double', which gained him the opportunity to indulge his unquenchable thirst for football knowledge at the 1954 World Cup Finals. That trip, more than anything else, probably opened his eager mind to wider possibilities that would stand him in good stead for the future.

When his playing days were brought to an untimely end by the ankle injury picked up against Rangers in the autumn of 1955, the unlikely on-field hero reverted to the coaching role that was the original purpose of his appointment. Working mainly with the reserves, he set about systematically revolutionising the Celtic training regime at that level. Within a couple of years, the resultant success of the second string had become a source of growing embarrassment to the top team, which, after the euphoria of '7-1', was struggling, as the ageing fifties heroes began to make way for younger blood towards the turn of the decade. Some of the players Stein would later 'inherit' (the so-called, 'Kelly Kids'), notably his future captain and on-field lieutenant, Billy McNeill, as well as the young Bertie Auld, in fact came under his influence around this time.

Season 1959/60 saw Jock branch out to begin cutting his managerial teeth, first at Dunfermline and then Hibernian - and what sharp teeth those proved to be!

The Stein magic quickly transformed the unfashionable Fifers from relegation fodder into one of Scotland's most formidable clubs, which went on to humble Celtic in the painful 1961 Scottish Cup Final. Following a goalless first game, Dunfermline ran out 2-0 winners in the replay, a superb tactical victory, undoubtedly governed by the recent 'inside knowledge' of a wily new manager. It has to be said, though, that the magnificent performances of Eddie Connaghan in the Dunfermline goal were decisive in both 'legs', particularly the replay, which will forever be remembered as 'The Connaghan Final'.

Having quickly established the 'Pars' as an unlikely force to be reckoned with in Scotland and led them proudly into Europe, Jock moved on in 1964 to a brief spell at Easter Road. There, he furthered an ever-growing reputation by immediately managing Hibs to victory in that year's Summer Cup; and when, as a parting gift, days before rejoining Celtic, they went on to knock Rangers out at the quarter-final stage of the following year's Scottish Cup, no further proof was needed. This man clearly had the Midas touch–and with the fruits of Bob Kelly's youth policy beginning to ripen, Celtic were sitting on a potential pot of gold.

The 'Second Coming'

By the time Jock Stein walked through the door of Celtic Park as manager on 9th March, 1965, his new charges were already sitting high and dry in the Scottish Cup semi-final, galvanised by the announcement on 31st January of the powerful wind of change about to blow through the club.

There was no acrimony this time, as there had been when Willie Maley was ousted and when Jimmy McStay was shoved aside to make way for Jimmy McGrory. In a carefully orchestrated operation, the messiah's path had been made straight in advance, ensuring a smooth transition with the full support of the faithful McGrory and *his* heir apparent prior to Stein's appointment, Sean Fallon. The legend-cum-manager was slotted in as Public Relations Officer, while the doughty fifties utility man readily agreed to stand aside and be his former team-mate's assistant.

Another key move had been made in the January, reputedly on Stein's say-so in advance of taking charge, through a sequence of contacts which suggest that his subsequent return to the Celtic fold dated back much further than was ever made public at the time. Bertie Auld, former victim of Bob Kelly's displeasure, as recounted earlier, was recalled from his Birmingham exile to bring his maturing influence and sometimes wayward genius to bear on the exciting but inexperienced young Celtic lions who had begun to show such rich promise. Names that would become legendary, like Murdoch, Johnstone, Gemmell and Lennox and others in danger of stagnation, such as McNeill, Chalmers, Clark and Gallagher lacked only the leadership, on the field and off, which came with the arrivals of Auld and Stein.

So, the scene was set fair for the day that would launch Celtic into a decade of dreams.

Scottish Cup Final, 24th April, 1965

Having disposed of traditionally formidable Scottish Cup adversaries, Motherwell, in the semi-final (3-0 in the replay of a 2-2 draw), Celtic and their new manager found themselves confronted in the final by Dunfermline Athletic. It was an ironic reversal of the situation when Stein had brought the Fifers to Hampden four years previously, so soon after taking over at East End Park.

On a blustery day, the infamous *'Hampden Swirl'* intensified rather than blighted an engrossing tussle, in which the 'Pars' drew first blood on the quarter-hour mark. Their captain, Harry Melrose, clipped the ball into an unguarded Celtic goal after 'keeper, John Fallon, had strayed from his line.

Celtic's first equaliser of the day in the thirty-first minute was a gem. A typical Charlie Gallagher drive struck the top of the Dunfermline crossbar and ballooned high into the air. The swirling wind swept the ball back down into play perilously near the post and little Bertie Auld, who had kept his eyes firmly fixed on its unpredictable trajectory, leapt fearlessly to outjump the mesmerised Dunfermline rearguard and head home.

Just when it seemed the interval would find the teams still locked at 1-1, Celtic took a last-minute body blow as Dunfermline went ahead again with a low drive by McLaughlin from a free-kick set-piece. How would Stein's troops respond to that?

The answer came in a storming second half, which was just six minutes old when Bobby Lennox and Bertie Auld combined to carve their way into the Fifers' box. The midfield general finished off the move by driving home his own and Celtic's second equaliser, the signal for a sustained barrage against an increasingly beleaguered black and white defensive wall.

Nine minutes from time, Lennox again played his part, forcing a left-side corner that would result in the day's decisive moment. A moment that would trigger the uncorked relief and unbridled joy of a support which, collectively, had either forgotten, or had never known, such rapture. As Billy McNeill's majestic header from Charlie Gallagher's measured cross flew into the net, seven years of acute frustration were washed away in a tide of realisation that Celtic had learned how to win again.

A momentary stunned silence erupted into a rising crescendo that seemed to gather decibels as it rolled around the old stadium, simultaneously acclaiming that day's deeds and heralding an as yet unknown but assuredly glorious future.

The Celtic heroes on a day which rang out the old and positively clanged in the new (simply listed, as the fluidity of the constantly evolving Stein systems would render strict positions increasingly obsolete), were:

Fallon: Young, Gemmell, Murdoch, McNeill, Clark, Chalmers, Gallagher, Hughes, Lennox & Auld.

Years later, Jock Stein, himself, would famously admit that the 1965 final was, indeed, a watershed and that subsequent events might have been very different had it gone the other way. As it was, he and Celtic were primed and ready to embark on a stupendous voyage of self-fulfilment.

Domestically, the following twelve seasons (eleven under Stein) saw Celtic amass ten League Championships, another seven Scottish Cups, six League Cups and four Glasgow Cups.

On the European front, a formidable reputation was established, beginning with the 1965/66 Cup Winners' Cup campaign, in which the now Scottish Cup *holders* emulated their 1963/64 'default' run to the semi-final. Along the way, they disposed of Go Ahead Deventer (Holland), Aarhus (Denmark) and Dinamo Kiev (former Soviet Union), scoring fourteen goals for the loss of only one. Such scorching form, so typical of the cavalier approach of Stein's Celtic, would, in time, inspire a French football columnist to dub them 'l'Orage' ('the Storm'), a splendidly succinct conceptualisation of their awesome attacking power. In the semi-final, the might of Liverpool prevailed, only because of a blatant refereeing error at Anfield, disallowing for offside a last-minute Bobby Lennox goal that would have taken Celtic into their first European final a year sooner. Lennox had actually carried the ball past a defender before slotting it behind the 'keeper. Not for the only time, the 'Buzz Bomb' was a victim of his own blinding pace, which on that occasion deceived the eye to Celtic's great cost.

In the same competition, 'Deputy' Sean Fallon took his squad to the quarter-final in Stein's enforced absence during the 1975/76 season.

The Champions' Cup record over the period was truly impressive – though not nearly as much so as it should have been, it has to be said. Two quarter finals (1968/69 and 1970/71), two semi finals (1971/72 and 1973/74) and two finals (1966/67 and 1969/70) is a creditable tally, it's true. The reality is, though, that Celtic's quality at that time should have brought the European Cup to the East End of Glasgow at least once more than it did, maybe more. However, to head off accusations of carping, let it be recorded here that the manner and circumstances of the legendary Lisbon triumph were such that it, alone, was more than enough to put the rightful stamp of immortality on the squad and manager who delivered it.

Days of Wine and Roses

It would be easy through the rose-tinted glasses of selective memory to imagine those Stein years as ones of continuous success. It was not so, as the aforementioned topsy-turvy League Cup record emphatically underlines.

All in all, though, the good times heavily outweighed the bad and at this safe distance in time, it is easy to indulge in pleasant reminiscence to the virtual exclusion of uncomfortable realities. They are there and the worst of them will never fade – but cool detachment and the collective memory's natural defences have long since taken care of most of them.

As the warm afterglow of 24th April, 1965 began to gently recede, the daunting prospect set in of future success being measured on a higher scale. Cups were one thing and that front was consolidated with the recapture of the League Cup in 1965/66, albeit none too convincingly in a rearguard 2-1 win over the ancient foe. Championships, though, were another matter entirely and while hefty league beatings were being liberally handed out, the 'signal' result was anxiously awaited.

It came in the displaced New Year 'derby' of 1966.

Celtic v Rangers, 3rd January, 1966

For more years than any Celtic person cared to remember, Rangers had been spoiling the party. Now, with the 'Old Firm' locked in mortal combat at the top of the table, having lost only one match apiece, they were threatening to do it again, just when things seemed to be looking up at last.

At a frozen Celtic Park, Rangers' blond left-winger, Davie Wilson, scored within two minutes and when the teams trooped off at the interval with Celtic still one down, it seemed like the age-old story. The palpable terracing unrest was the product of fans who had dared to believe their time had come, sensing that the bitter pill of shattered dreams might have to be swallowed yet again. The dread of anti-climax hung heavy in the air and the awful prospect of renewed gloating in Govan loomed large.

But this was not a Celtic that would wilt in the face of adversity or meekly bend the knee to Rangers hegemony. It *was* a resilient new Celtic, after all. A Celtic steeped in the faith that is born of unshakeable confidence, each in himself, collectively in each other and above all in a remarkable new leader – *and this was to be their day.*

The second half became a triumphal march, a joyous proclamation of Celtic's rediscovered pride and the accompanying shift of power from Copland Road to Kerrydale Street.

With the mighty John Hughes running amok on the treacherous surface, Steve Chalmers sounded the charge in the fiftieth minute with the kind of goal that would become a Celtic trademark under Stein. Converting a cutback from the by-line by overlapping fullback, Tommy Gemmell, Stevie went on to complete his 'hat-trick' in a 5-1 rout, with Bobby Murdoch and Charlie Gallagher grabbing the other two.

It was a good day to be a Celtic man, because any lingering half-time doubt about the likely course of events for the foreseeable future was blown clear across the Clyde in the direction of

Dressing room celebrations after clinching the 1965/66 title at Motherwell on 7th May, 1966.

Ibrox Stadium by that spellbinding second forty-five minutes.

The destination of the league flag now seemed a foregone conclusion, although it wouldn't be finally clinched until the 1-0 victory at Fir Park, Motherwell, on Saturday, 7th May, 1966. What a day *that* was, as Celtic claimed their first title in twelve long years, setting the seal on a breakthrough season, distinguished by two major trophies and the above massive psychological boost against the old enemy.

Even the disappointment of missing out on a glorious 'treble' by dint of losing unluckily to Rangers by the only goal of a replayed (initially goalless) 1966 Scottish Cup Final could not take the gloss off a truly historic term that set up the forthcoming 'Season of Seasons'.

A Season in the Sun

The *tour de force* that was season 1966/67, comprehensively portrayed in an earlier book whose title was borrowed for this section, was preceded by a long summer tour of the United States and Canada. That North American safari is widely accredited as the wellspring of the indomitable team spirit which swept the squad to legendary feats on its return.

Whether it really was the bonding effect of that trip or just something in the Parkhead water in those days, Celtic were unstoppable that season. Boosted by the thrilling 4-1 pre-season 'friendly' demolition of a star-studded Manchester United, the three domestic cups (League, Scottish and Glasgow), as well as the retained Championship, were wrapped up in scintillating style. There really was, in those immortal words of Paul McStay, *"a buzz about the place."* (Did he *really* say that, or was it just his *'Only An Excuse'* caricature?)

'Goin tae the gemme' was sheer joy. It wasn't a case of, "D'ye think we'll win the day?" More, "How many d'ye think we'll win by?" And that wasn't complacency, simply a well-founded conviction that, no matter what the opposition did, Celtic would do that bit more. Usually, quite a lot more.

The real story of 1966/67, though, was, of course, Europe and Celtic's first foray into the Champions' Cup. The team had performed heroically a couple of times in the Cup Winners' Cup but this was the 'real deal', in among the big boys. The Champions' Cup seemed to be the exclusive domain of the Latin maestros of Spain, Italy and Portugal. No non-Latin club had ever won it. No British team had ever even reached the final. It was the Everest of the football world and Celtic were at base camp without a Sherpa. On the other hand, they did have Jock Stein – and a squad of players on the threshold of greatness who had ripped up the script.

The Glory Run

The passage was fairly straightforward as far as the quarter final, reached via 5-0 and 6-2 aggregates against the Swiss and French champions, Zurich and Nantes, respectively. It was a different story altogether, though, from there on in.

Vojvodina Novi Sad, champions of (former) Yugoslavia, presented a stern test in the last eight and possibly the tensest night ever at Celtic Park. Ahead 1-0 from the first leg, thanks to a moment of defensive rashness by Tommy Gemmell, the robust, skilful Slavs had Celtic reeling in an unusually lacklustre, goalless first half back in Glasgow. Even after the break, when Celtic got their act together and exerted real pressure, it seemed as if the visitors might hold out to thwart the revival and progress to the semi final. Then Gemmell made amends for his first-leg brainstorm by tempting goalkeeper, Pantelic, into a crucial misjudgement that resulted in Stevie Chalmers sweeping home the equaliser.

Thereafter, despite a mounting Celtic assault, it began to look, as the rules then stood, as if a play-off would be required to decide the tie. Then, as the game crept into the dying moments, the last in a series of late Celtic corners was forced on the right flank. Charlie Gallagher drew gasps of dismay from the supporters, as he appeared to dither over the kick with the final whistle due any second. In fact, though, the dead-ball expert knew exactly what he was doing, having spotted Billy McNeill positioning himself for a late run. The kick, when it came, hung perfectly for 'Caesar' to send a looping header into the net for the most dramatic winner imaginable. There was barely time left for the stunned Yugoslavs to re-centre the ball and the tumultuous roar of relief and exultation that greeted McNeill's goal had scarcely subsided as the referee brought the match to an end. It really was as close as that. Of all the tension-filled nights that would follow in years to come, few, if any, would equal and certainly none would surpass that one for sheer nerve-jangling tension and crackling atmosphere.

The semi final against the renowned Czechoslovakian Army team and national champions, Dukla Prague, was equally formidable, if rather less dramatic. Led by the masterly Josef Masopust, who had captained his country to the World Cup Final of 1962, in Chile, Dukla tested Celtic to the limit in Glasgow before going down 3-1 to a quicksilver Jimmy Johnstone opening strike and a Willie Wallace double.

Such was the wariness and respect generated by the Czechs' performance that, to his later embarrassment, Big Jock for once abandoned his attacking instincts and ordered an uncharacteristic all-out rearguard action for the return leg, in the pursuit of a historic first British qualification for a Champions' Cup Final.

Mission accomplished, however unattractively.

European Cup Final, 1967

Celtic came to Lisbon's Estadio Nacional on 25th May, 1967 as clear underdogs. Twice former winners, Inter Milan, were thoroughbreds and nobody outwith the Scottish Champions' camp gave them much of a chance.

However, a massive travelling support and overwhelming local backing in the run-up to and on the day, handed Celtic a crucial psychological advantage to back up their intrinsic self-confidence. Even the potentially crushing blow of falling behind to an early penalty would not deter them. In the final analysis, the alleged Scottish no-hopers totally dominated their superstar rivals and the slender 2-1 margin of victory was an utter travesty.

Tommy Gemmell's sixty-third minute equaliser is etched forever in the collective Celtic memory, as he thundered Jim Craig's perfect pass behind the previously inspired Sarti in the Inter goal. The European Cup was won there and then, though Steve Chalmers' clinching strike did not come for another twenty minutes or so.

As the final whistle sounded and ecstatic Celtic hordes streamed onto the pitch to pay homage at the shrine, the enormity of what they had just witnessed began to sink in, just as it did throughout the Celtic 'family' across the world. A team of homebred Scots, inheritors and trustees of Walfrid's dream, had borne the hopes and aspirations of successive generations to an unprecedented pinnacle. Their Everest had been conquered and no-one could ever take that supreme moment from them.

Billy McNeill with European Cup during the Celtic Park homecoming 'Gala Night' on 26th May, 1967.

Good days, even great days, would not be in short supply as the coming years unfolded – but the day that spawned *'The Lisbon Lions'* would never be surpassed:

Simpson: Craig, Gemmell, Murdoch, McNeill, Clark, Johnstone, Wallace, Chalmers, Auld & Lennox.

The Lisbon Legacy

The trouble with landmark seasons like 1966/67 and supreme episodes such as the Lisbon final is that things can never be quite the same again. The subsequent Stein years, for all their continuing distinction, illustrated by the table at the end of this section, laboured against that simple reality.

Glory aplenty awaited successive Celtic squads under Big Jock's guidance and every fan who shared those special years has his or her own favourite recollections. Prominent amongst most of those are sure to be one or more of the following:

● Alfredo di Stefano Testimonial

ON 7th June, 1967, Celtic had their new status as European Champions tested in the fiercest of fires against their immediate predecessors, Real Madrid, in the Spaniards' Bernabeu Stadium. Jimmy Johnstone chose that magnificent venue to stage a virtuoso performance of his inimitable skills and Celtic's honour was upheld in a 1-0 victory. Bobby Lennox slotted home the winner, inevitably set up by the irrepressible 'Jinky'.

● Celtic 5, Red Star Belgrade 1

THE 1968/69 European Cup campaign produced one of the greatest nights ever at Celtic Park. Johnstone again took centre stage as he ripped Red Star to shreds in a pulsating second half. A classic piece of Stein psychology did the trick, capitalising on the 'Wee Man's' fear of flying by promising not to take him on the 'away' leg if a four-goal lead was achieved at home.

● Scottish Cup Final, 1969

THIS joyous 4-0 hammering of Rangers has to be one of the sweetest moments of all. Billy McNeill headed Celtic into the lead in only the second minute, steering the ball in off the post from a corner on the left. Just before half time, a devastating one-two from Bobby Lennox and George Connelly really sunk the 'Gers and Steve Chalmers rounded it all off in the second half with an astonishing, long angled run in on goal to stab home number four.

● European Cup Semi Final, 1970

LEEDS UTD were unbeatable that year (according to the English press, that is) and Celtic were dismissed in very derogatory terms by some. One particularly arrogant scribe rated their latest Championship win of no more significance than the outcome of the Boat Race. Imagine his chagrin when Celtic turned United over 'home' and 'away' in titanic struggles at Elland Road (1-0) and Hampden (2-1) to reach their second European Cup Final. Sadly, because they were a great team in their own right, 'unbeatable' Leeds were so demoralised that they proceeded to stumble, both in the league run-in and in the F.A. Cup, ending up with nothing.

● Scottish Cup Final, 1972

OVER the period, Hibs suffered grievously at Celtic's hands in cup finals, belying their genuine quality at that time. The League Cups of 1968 and 1974 brought respective 6-2 and 6-3 hidings. This great Scottish Cup Final also cost them six goals, as centre-forward, 'Dixie' Deans notched only the second 'hat-trick' ever in the premier national final, emulating Jimmy Quinn's feat of 1904. Hibs managed only one in reply.

Days of Reckoning

On the other side of the coin, though mercifully very much in the minority, there were times when even Stein's wizardry could not prevent a salutary dose of harsh reality. Such instances, always painful and often embarrassing, were unwelcome reminders that Celtic had no more divine right to supremacy than anyone else, even at a time when such an elitist attitude could almost be forgiven.

Without seeking to re-open old wounds, let us never forget:

- THE anger and remorse generated by the shameful events *provoked* by the 1967 World Club Championship series against Racing Club of Argentina.
- THE deep depression and disillusioned bewilderment at the manner and circumstances of the 1970 European Cup Final defeat by Feyenoord at the San Siro Stadium in Milan.
- THE acute shock and embarrassment of the 4-1 humbling by a youthful Partick Thistle in the League Cup Final of 1971.

Let's leave it at that, or we're liable to turn maudlin and have Big Jock spinning in his grave.

Players

In a very different football ethos from today, the players who brought so much honour on Celtic under Jock Stein were, in the main, Scottish and with a few notable exceptions, the product of the club's own internal breeding system.

As with recollection of events, individual assessment and appreciation of players is inevitably subjective – in any era. For example, ask a hundred fans what they think of, say, Tommy Callaghan, or, more recently, Peter Grant, Paul McStay or Regi Blinker and you are guaranteed a rich variety of opinion.

Certainly, though, during the Stein Years, there was much to admire:

- THE commanding leadership and aerial dominance of Billy McNeill.
- THE midfield guile and craft of Bobby Murdoch and Bertie Auld.
- THE strike power of Joe McBride, Willie Wallace and 'Dixie' Deans.
- THE pace, courage and skill of that doyen of fullbacks, Danny McGrain.
- THE all-round class of the peerless Kenny Dalglish.
- THE elegant but sadly wayward genius of troubled George Connelly.

. . . the list could go on and on. By way of collective tribute, then, to all the great players of a golden era, take a moment to reflect on the immortal memory of the most distinctive of them all.

Jimmy Johnstone

Considered by many the greatest Scottish football talent of living memory and unquestionably the most unique, 'Jinky' was the brightest jewel in Jock Stein's crown and the sharpest thorn in his flesh. Their at times uneasy alliance prospered out of mutual respect, dedication to the club and Stein's ability to coax, cajole, bribe and if necessary, terrorise Jimmy into toeing the line and producing his inimitable brand of genius for Celtic.

Johnstone lit up Scottish and European football with his mesmerising control, darting runs and bewildering changes of pace and direction, at times seeming, like John Thomson before him, to defy the very laws of physics in the process. His uncanny skill and fearless heart made Jimmy a matchwinner, at times single-handedly and inflicted the roasting of a lifetime on more than a few shell-shocked world-class opponents.

He is remembered with awe and affection.

The Stein Record

SEASON	League	Sco. Cup	L'ge Cup	Gl'w Cup	ECWC	UEFA	Euro.Cup
1964/65	N/A	Winners	N/A	N/A	N/A	N/A	N/A
1965/66	Winners	Final	Winners		Semi-final	N/A	N/A
1966/67	Winners	Winners	Winners	Winners	N/A	N/A	Winners
1967/68	Winners	Round 1	Winners	Winners	N/A	N/A	Round 1
1968/69	Winners	Winners	Winners		N/A	N/A	Q-final
1969/70	Winners	Final	Winners	Winners	N/A	N/A	Final
1970/71	Winners	Winners	Final		N/A	N/A	Q-final
1971/72	Winners	Winners	Final		N/A	N/A	Semi-final
1972/73	Winners	Final	Final		N/A	N/A	Round 2
1973/74	Winners	Winners	Final		N/A	N/A	Semi-final
1974/75	Third	Winners	Winners	Jt Winner	N/A	N/A	Round 1
1975/76	Second	Round 3	Final		Q-final	N/A	N/A
1976/77	Winners	Winners	Final		N/A	Round 1	N/A
1977/78	Fifth	Round 4	Final		N/A	N/A	Round 2

1964/65   ***Jock Stein only took over from Jimmy McGrory on 9th March, 1965.***

1975/76   ***Sean Fallon deputised for Jock Stein due to severe car crash injuries.***

After such distinguished service as player and manager, the circumstances of Jock's departure in 1978 were nothing short of diabolical. By contrast with the meticulously engineered harmony of his arrival to succeed Jimmy McGrory, confusion was allowed to surround the exact nature of the 'executive directorship' offered and it became widely perceived, rightly or wrongly, as a snub to one of Celtic's most prominent figures. Whatever the truth of the matter, a Celtic icon, who should have been cherished in the manner of Matt Busby at Manchester United, left within a few months, disgruntled and apparently rejected, to take up the managerial reins at Leeds United.

No matter, the golden legacy of Jock Stein's proud association with the club he learned to love and served with such distinction can never be diminished and will long outlive the memory of those who ultimately served him so shabbily.

'Caesar' & 'The Quiet Assassin': Billy McNeill / David Hay (1978 - 1991)

BILLY McNEILL, having led Celtic with distinction for so long on the field, retired as player and Club Captain after the Scottish Cup Final win over Airdrie in 1975. Just over three years later, following a brief spell out of football and early managerial experience with Clyde and Aberdeen, he received the offer he simply couldn't refuse. He would return to Celtic Park as successor to the man who had been his mentor for so many years, taking over from Jock Stein in time for the start of season 1978/79.

This first term of his split managership would ultimately prove successful, yielding three Championships, one Scottish Cup, one League Cup and a Glasgow Cup in the space of five years. It began unconvincingly, though, coinciding with the insensitive mishandling of Stein's departure.

Perhaps over-zealousness in his determination to set out his stall caused him to take his eye off that particular ball. Certainly, subsequent comments attributed to Billy suggested he felt that maybe he could have done more to help Big Jock reconcile himself to life at Celtic Park in a less prominent position. More to assuage the inevitable sense of rejection his former boss would be feeling in those early days away from the 'sharp end'. To be fair, though, he was, himself, under immediate pressure to begin charting a course back to winning ways and nobody would thank him for any failure on that front as a result of time devoted to easing his predecessor's path into retirement. He had his own place in Celtic history to look to and couldn't be held accountable for dubious goings on outwith his sphere of influence.

So he busied himself in the transfer market, having from the outset made it clear that money would have to be spent quickly. In came winger, Davie Provan, from Kilmarnock and midfielder, Murdo MacLeod, from Dumbarton, for £120,000 and £100,000 respectively, small beer by today's standards but significant sums in the great Celtic scheme of things at the time. Veteran 'Lisbon Lion', Bobby Lennox, was recalled from his exile in the United States to reinforce the attack.

Any hopes McNeill may have harboured that things would be turned around quickly were soon dashed. Poor early league form was aggravated by defeat at the hands of Rangers in the League Cup. Uncustomarily without a place in Europe, the non-event that was the *Anglo-Scottish Cup* brought embarrassing defeat by Burnley and things were looking really bad.

Big Billy needed a 'break' and he got one – an extended one, as severe winter weather shut down Scottish football until March!

By the time play resumed, the influential Danny McGrain, who was plagued by illness and serious injury throughout his courageous career, was back as captain after an *eighteen-month* absence. Remarkably, despite the shaky early season, Celtic were still in the hunt, as no-one had really asserted themselves in the league. Aberdeen ended Scottish Cup interest but with the interrupted programme extended into May, two results that month set up a thrilling end to the season.

Rangers' 1-0 success early in the month made them favourites for the title, a point clear with four games remaining. However, by the time the pair met again for Celtic's final fixture (Rangers still had another two games to play), the three intervening victories meant that full points would take the Championship to Celtic Park, irrespective of what followed.

Celtic v Rangers, 21st May, 1979

The story of this game is really the story of a remarkable second half. The old cliché about things having to get worse before they get better has seldom been more clearly demonstrated, as Celtic found themselves with their backs well and truly against the wall.

Rangers resumed after the interval 1-0 ahead and the fiery Johnny Doyle got sent off for retaliation early in the second half. A substitution brought on Bobby Lennox for Conroy and all-out attack was the order of the day. There was really no alternative.

How handsomely it paid off, too. Roy Aitken levelled the match with a header that caused bedlam on the terracing and the frenzy intensified when George McCluskey fired Celtic into the lead with fifteen minutes remaining. That last quarter of an hour was like an eternity. The dream seemed to be snatched away as Rangers promptly equalised and it seemed their manpower advantage might prevail.

That was when 'Lady Luck' chose to smile on Celtic, as a Jackson own-goal swung the pendulum back their way and stunned Rangers with just seven minutes left on the clock. If the 'Hoops' could hold firm, a sensational title win would be theirs but the tension was almost unbearable. One slip and it could all end in tears. The 'Kleenex' was not required, though.

Murdo MacLeod had cost £100,000 but the strike he produced in the final minute was priceless. His long-range shot tore into the net, high and behind the towering Peter McCloy to settle the issue and repay the manager's faith with interest.

McNeill had done it, against all odds and how the fans hailed their 'Caesar'. His gladiators at Celtic Park that day were:

Latchford: McGrain, Lynch, Aitken, McAdam, Edvaldsson, Provan, Conroy (Lennox), McCluskey, MacLeod & Doyle.

Season 1979/80 brought the disappointment of quarter-final defeat by Aberdeen in the League Cup but in the league, things started well and the turn of the year found Celtic out in front.

Progress was good, too, in the European Cup. Despite a one-goal deficit from the 'away' first leg of the first-round tie against Partizan Tirana of Albania, the tables were turned in Glasgow with a 4-1 win and a subsequent 3-2 aggregate victory over Irish champions, Dundalk, set up a dream quarter final against Real Madrid.

Unfortunately, that's where the whole season started to go wrong, although an eight-point lead had been built up in the league by the time the Spanish maestros came calling.

Despite laying out a then Scottish record fee of £250,000 to bring Frank McGarvey from Liverpool and establishing a 2-0 first-leg lead in Glasgow on 5th March, 1980, the loss of an early goal in Madrid a fortnight later was the start of a disastrous night that ended in defeat by 3-0. Out 3-2 on aggregate, things began to go downhill rapidly.

The aftershock carried over into the league, which slipped away from a seemingly unassailable position. The only consolation was a sweet 1-0 victory over Rangers in the Scottish Cup Final. Even that, though, went sour when a joyous incursion onto the pitch by celebrating Celtic supporters was challenged by a menacing charge from the other end of the stadium. The result was an ugly pitched battle for which both clubs, in the classic S.F.A. manner of 'even-handedness' over such incidents, irrespective of circumstances, were fined equally. The victorious Celts were:

Latchford: Sneddon, McGrain, Aitken, Conroy, MacLeod, Provan, Doyle, McCluskey, Burns & McGarvey.

It had been a season of cruel anti-climax, in which even the good times were bad.

Decline and Fall

Despite back-to-back titles in 1980/81 and 1981/82, giving McNeill an enviable record of three Championships in four seasons, the seeds of his eventual downfall were sown early in his third term (1980/81).

A simmering feud behind the scenes would lead to a progressive degeneration in his relationship with Chairman, Desmond White. The ambitious, headstrong manager and the cautious, calculating supremo could not see eye-to-eye over financial policy and its knock-on effect into football operations. All too often, Billy appeared to be trying, directly or indirectly, to harness his huge public popularity to swing the argument his way. There could be only one winner, though – and it was never likely to be the football man. Taken together with a series of disciplinary matters, McNeill's position became steadily undermined in his three-year 'tug-o-war' with White and the board.

On the football front, things were comparatively buoyant by the standards of most clubs, though the cup record was less than impressive. Only the Glasgow Cup of 1981/82 and the 1982/83 League Cup found their way to 'Paradise'. On the other hand, there were those back-to-back league titles to point to and the emergence of precocious talents such as Charlie Nicholas and Paul McStay.

Nicholas and Murdo MacLeod scored the goals that snatched the League Cup from Rangers on 4th December, 1982 to secure the first major silverware of 1982/83. That season also saw a startling 4-3 aggregate European Cup win over Johann Cruyff's

Ajax, in which George McCluskey grabbed a glorious winner in Amsterdam after a 2-2 draw at Celtic Park.

It was not enough, though, to stave off the mounting 'backstage' problems, which came to a head in June, 1983. That month witnessed the curious 'McCoist' affair, which might, it seems, have taken the legendary Rangers 'hit-man' to Celtic instead but the chance, such as it was, slipped away with McNeill on holiday. Charlie Nicholas opted for the bright lights of London, with Arsenal and Brian McClair arrived from Motherwell.

The latter part of the month found the manager and club locked in another very public wrangle over his terms and lack of contract in the wake of reported interest in his services from Manchester City. It was one 'open debate' too many and led to the parting of the ways. Following a terse confrontation with the board in White's city offices, McNeill joined the Manchester 'blues'.

It was over – for now. 'Caesar' still had a part to play, though, and the prodigal would return.

DAVID HAY had been a fine player for Celtic, having graduated from the same post-Lisbon school of excellence that produced the likes of McGrain, Dalglish, Macari and Connelly. Hard (*very* hard – just ask John Greig) but fair, his sometime nickname, 'The Quiet Assassin', with its misleading sinister undertones, was something of a misnomer and belied the quiet, thoughtful, laid-back approach of the future manager.

His installation as successor to Billy McNeill on 4th July, 1983 was, given his modest managerial experience, more an act of faith in a former stalwart (notwithstanding his acceptance of the Chelsea shilling) than the shrewd appointment of a 'coming man'. It was ultimately to prove faith misplaced, as Hay's tenure proved to be one of ever-heightening unease in supporters. They and the directors could see former glories fading fast in the face of uncustomary challenges from the east and north in the shape of the 'New Firm' of Dundee United and Aberdeen. Rangers, of course, hadn't gone away, either.

It is not that everything was doom and gloom. There were a lot of good players around like Burns, McClair, McStay, McGarvey and Provan. There was, of course, also Maurice Johnston, the least said about whom the better, brought back to Scotland from Watford for £400,000 (another Scottish record fee). Yet there was an inescapable sense of drift, of a lack of discipline and direction. Second prizes seemed to be the order of the day, or else Celtic weren't even in the shakedown.

Hay's position was not helped by the Rapid Vienna fiasco in the Cup Winners' Cup of 1984/85, which plunged Celtic into even deeper depression than did the bleak domestic scenario. The awful events, and punitive aftermath of that debacle, had extensive repercussions. Celtic were eliminated from the competition, suffered a financial penalty and had a 'closed doors' order imposed for their next 'home' European tie (which effectively contributed to Celtic's demise in the same event the following year, against Atletico Madrid).

That David Hay survived the smouldering unrest of those unhappy times for so long was largely due to two unlikely successes. Although most welcome and offering merciful relief from the general air of disaffection, the Scottish Cup victory of 1985 and the following season's league success temporarily papered over cracks which would soon develop into the major fault lines that would trigger the return of 'Caesar'.

The fact that the 1985 final was the climax of the 100th Scottish Cup added spice to the occasion and furthered Celtic's romantic reputation for producing the goods on big occasions, as often as not in the midst of turmoil.

A goal down to Dundee United with just under quarter of an hour to go, Celtic seemed dead and buried until Davie Provan's dead-ball expertise produced a spectacular free kick equaliser. We had seen it all before and it came as no surprise at all when Frank McGarvey languidly diverted Roy Aitken's cross into the net with his head for the winner five or six minutes from the final whistle. The winning line-up was:

Bonner: W. McStay, McGrain, Aitken, McAdam, MacLeod, Provan, P. McStay, Johnston, Burns & McGarvey.

When the immediate euphoria had passed, though, the majority of Celtic supporters were well aware that the welcome crumb of comfort was just that and not a 'New Dawn'. Nevertheless, the following season was to prolong the illusion of resurgence for anyone minded to perceive it.

Last Day Snatch

Season 1985/86 held little to quell the mounting frustrations of the previous two years but it would come to an enthralling climax.

The various cup campaigns were uninspiring. Hibs did the damage at the quarter-final stage of both domestic competitions. The 'Rapid' hangover contributed to UEFA Cup exit, as mentioned earlier.

The league was something of a dogfight. Hearts were the predominant front-runners, without ever managing to shake off the pack completely. So it was that Celtic's strong finish, allied to 'Jambo' jitters in the run-in, resulted in a final day when the title was still up for grabs, with Hearts in the driving seat.

Celtic had to go to Paisley more in hope than expectation, while Hearts were 'away' to Dundee, needing only a draw to clinch the title. The outside chance of an upset lay in a high-scoring Celtic win over St Mirren (a three-goal victory, or better, was the target) and a Hearts defeat. Let's just say the 'smart money' wasn't on Celtic!

However, McClair (2), Johnston (2) and McStay had fired the 'Hoops' into a 5-0 lead by ten minutes into the second half and suddenly there were possibilities. It was a blistering performance that showed just what the team was capable of on a good day.

Attention then turned to events on Tayside. As the goal reports filtered through on transistor radios, there was momentary anxiety as to which 'Kidd' was doing the scoring, particularly at the second strike. Could it be a dreaded equaliser? No. It was Dundee's Albert, not Hearts' Walter, on both occasions. The unabashed Celtic fan had struck a late double – and Celtic were Champions.

The tumultuous celebrations were an outpouring of disbelief as much as of joy. But a Championship is a Championship and it was there to be enjoyed. Sometimes the best parties are the surprise ones.

In the midst of it all, the manager, admittedly never the most demonstrative guy in the world, was strangely subdued.

Endgame

Hay's final season was nightmarish. It didn't help that a Scottish football revolution was getting underway on the other side of the city, with the arrival at Ibrox of Graeme Souness.

All the cups slipped away again – the League Cup at the final stage to that rampant new Rangers, the Scottish Cup against Hearts (4th Round) and the European Cup at the hands of Dinamo Kiev (2nd Round). Worse still, in the league, a *ten-point* lead established by December in a long unbeaten run, was foozled away and the title was destined for Ibrox.

The writing was on the wall. Serious doubt set in about Hay's ability to hold onto key players, several of whose contracts were up for renewal. Something had to give.

All this coincided with renewed turmoil in Billy McNeill's career, which had gone rapidly downhill in England. Unhappy episodes at Manchester City and Aston Villa had left him out of a job and considering a range of unattractive options.

Meanwhile, after months of deliberation, the Celtic board had decided he was their man. The deal to turn back the clock and restore the club's favourite son was thrashed out by McNeill and the latest Chairman, Jack McGinn, in the now infamous clandestine Clydebank car park meeting, while Billy was in Scotland for a 'Lisbon Lions' reunion.

On the morning of 28th May, 1987, David Hay was offered the chance to resign, refused and was sacked. That evening, Billy McNeill was dramatically unveiled as the 'new' manager of Celtic.

Centenary Glory

The story of Billy McNeill's second term is, essentially, the story of the 'Centenary Double'. Confronted by the emerging new order of things across the city and never one to shirk a challenge, 'Caesar' knew only too well the importance of the 'landmark' season that lay ahead. Surely, the football gods could not shun Celtic at such a momentous point in time – but recent history offered little prospect of a happy hundredth birthday.

Summer reconstruction brought striker Andy Walker from Motherwell, fullback, Chris Morris, from Sheffield Wednesday and experienced midfielder, Billy Stark, from

Aberdeen. The new men would slot in around Davie Hay's last signing, rugged Republic of Ireland centre-half, Mick McCarthy and the emerging young talent of Derek Whyte.

'Friendly' defeats, a truly disheartening pre-season 5-1 mauling by Arsenal and a single-goal reverse in the Tommy Burns testimonial by Kenny Dalglish's Liverpool, did nothing to encourage fresh optimism. Despite the boost of a 1-0 'home' win in the first 'Old Firm' league clash, the September exits from both the League and UEFA Cups highlighted attacking deficiencies. These were addressed by the acquisition of West Ham's ex-St Mirren striker, Frank McAvennie and winger, Joe Miller, from Aberdeen – and the final seeds of glory had been sown.

From third place in the league behind Aberdeen and Hearts in early October, an amazing surge took Celtic to the top of the table by the end of November. The continuation of a thirty-one game unbeaten run, extending from the 2-1 defeat by Dundee United on 24th October, 1987 until 16th April, 1988 at Tynecastle, included the 2-0 New Year 'Old Firm' triumph at Celtic Park that signalled genuine title prospects.

A nostalgic diversion from serious league business had come when former hero, Kenny Dalglish, by then manager of Liverpool, donned the 'hoops' once more as a substitute in the Davie Provan testimonial v Nottingham Forest on 30th November, 1987. It was a typically touching moment in keeping with Celtic's 'family' tradition.

The decisive game of that season was undoubtedly the televised league fixture at Ibrox on 20th March, 1988. Celtic confounded the pundits that day by launching an all-out attack which yielded a 2-1 win and a six-point lead to cushion the league run-in, rather than playing for the draw which would have consolidated their position at the top.

Even the Hearts defeat, which brought a halt to the thrilling title surge, turned out to be more of a favour than a setback. It meant that the League Championship would be clinched the following Saturday in a 3-0 victory over Dundee at Celtic Park, lauded by a delirious rendition of 'Happy Birthday to Celtic'. The Scottish Cup then beckoned and with it, the prospect of a Centenary feat unimaginable during the dark days of such recent memory.

The early stages of the cup had been as uninspiring as the opening to the league campaign. Lowly Stranraer were only narrowly seen off 1-0 at Celtic Park, having scorned the opportunity of taking Celtic to an embarrassing replay by missing a penalty. Hibs were beaten 1-0 after a goalless draw, Partick Thistle somewhat more comfortably at Firhill with goals from Walker, Burns and Stark.

The semi final against Hearts had a truly stunning finale, which smacked of destiny. Trailing 1-0 in the dying minutes, Celtic dug deep into the reservoir of inspirational club tradition to hit the 'Jambos' with a last-gasp double kick in the teeth from Mark McGhee and Andy Walker.

'Centenary' Cup Final

Saturday, 14th May, 1988 was the stuff of dreams. It was in a carnival atmosphere that Celtic took the field against Dundee United at a sun-drenched Hampden. The 'Saharan' weather appeared to favour the Tayside 'Arabs' but the Celtic 'faithful', still wallowing in Championship euphoria, seemed curiously unperturbed by traditionally dangerous opponents.

The first half produced little to dispel the serenity of it all but early in the second, the illusion of inevitability was shattered. Kevin (grandson of Patsy) Gallacher ran away from a hesitant Roy Aitken (who had earlier been booked for a foul on the same player) to flash a high drive behind a rather static Allen McKnight, who was deputising for the injured Pat Bonner. Suddenly, Celtic were struggling, seemingly trapped in lethargy, and the dream was fading fast.

It was time for 'Caesar' to play the imperious role his alias implied. He did just that, turning the game around with a masterly double substitution. Mark McGhee brought some much-needed urgency up front, while Billy Stark took midfield control.

The equaliser came from a McAvennie header to convert a Rogan cross with fifteen minutes to go. You could almost taste the huge relief of the Celtic hordes, who would probably have settled there and then for extra time ... but this was not a day for delaying the course of history.

Frank McAvennie stamped his name indelibly in the pages of Celtic folklore with his own second of the day and the winner. 'Macca' joyously fired the ball home as it broke to him five yards out, dead in front of goal, in practically the last attack of the game, following a late Joe Miller corner on the right.

Suddenly, it was all over, as the final whistle which brought the curtain down on a glorious Celtic century became the fanfare for an unlikely 'Centenary Double' and that day's heroes:

McKnight: Morris, Rogan, Aitken, McCarthy, Whyte, (Stark), Miller, McStay, McAvennie, Walker, (McGhee) & Burns.

It was really all over then for Billy McNeill, too. Although he would be in charge for a further three seasons and add the 1988/89 Scottish Cup to his tally, things never could or would be the same again, as a smothering light blue blanket settled on Scottish football and Celtic fortunes.

He walked away, perhaps at times bloodied but certainly unbowed by the controversies of his comings and goings, leaving behind a gleaming legacy of silverware, including thirteen League Championships (9 as player and 14 as manager) as his epitaph.

'Back from the Brink' (1991-1998)

THE EARLY NINETIES found Celtic in the throes of one of the blackest periods in their history, a period that would ultimately bring them once again to the edge of oblivion. On this occasion though, unlike in the fifties with the 'flag' affair, the threat came not from malevolent external forces but from within.

Those years were characterised by bitter in-fighting, as the old board fought to stave off mounting criticism of their alleged mismanagement, self-interest and incompetence. The club lurched from one crisis to the next, unsure, even, where the team's future lay and faced with the unpalatable prospect of being uprooted from the spiritual homeland of Celtic Park. Unpalatable to most fans, anyway – but what did they matter? That washed-up old board would soon find out.

"Save Our Celts!", was the order of the day. "Sack the Board!", became the battle cry, as supporters mobilised and potential takeover consortia closed in to attempt to avert disaster and re-direct the club. The sad scenario would lead inevitably to that dark day in early 1994 when it took a last-ditch financial salvage operation by Fergus McCann to snatch Celtic back from the brink and dramatically change the face of the club.

Before that, though, against this depressing scenario, Celtic had to find a way to combat the Rangers juggernaut that was gathering momentum alarmingly. With a view, presumably, to fighting fire with fire, it was decided to replace Billy McNeill with a figure of international standing. Someone to spark the imagination and with the 'clout' to attract the sort of big names that would restore credibility and competitiveness.

The man appointed was Liam Brady. He certainly had the international standing, having been a player of rare talent at both club and international level. Whether he fitted the other criteria is debatable but one thing is certain. Brady never fully grasped what it was to *be* Celtic manager, particularly at that time. He didn't seem to understand the passion of the whole thing. It was as if it didn't really *matter* that Celtic were languishing while their major rivals went from strength to strength and began to disappear over the horizon.

In short, he was the wrong man for the job, as two fruitless seasons were to prove and it was time to think again.

So, they thought again and having thought, decided it was time to go back to the club's roots. Appoint a 'Celtic man'. One with managerial credentials and everything would fall into place. The thinking may not have been quite as basic as that but essentially that's what it boiled down to.

The man appointed was Lou Macari. A 'Celtic man', certainly, though not for all that long before taking himself off to Manchester to devote his maturing talents to the United cause. His managerial credentials were hardly of the highest order but to be fair, he had a record of success and everyone has to start out somewhere. His arrival was greeted with mixed feelings but the majority probably felt that here was someone they could, at least, identify with and who would be given a fair chance.

Lou had his moments of glory, notably his competitive debut in the stunning 2-1 victory at Ibrox in October, 1993. Overall, though, there was a curious air of unfamiliarity haunting the club under Macari and his henchmen (it would later be suggested that Lou was never around long enough to *become* familiar) – and things weren't really getting any better.

In short, he was probably the wrong man for the job, too, though he didn't get much opportunity to prove otherwise. Macari was overtaken by events, as Fergus McCann took control in March, 1994, following the takeover that swept the boardroom clear of the 'old guard' who had dragged Celtic so perilously close to ruin.

Unfortunately, the aftermath of litigation and bad blood that followed the dismissal of Lou Macari was the precursor of the sort of hostile internal feuding and general siege mentality that was to become an all-too-typical feature of the post-takeover regime at Celtic Park. The ensuing years have thrown up a succession of public issues involving players, management and backroom staff which, in some cases, have left fans variously hurt, angered and bewildered.

Share Issue

Following the 1994 revolution, Fergus McCann quickly fulfilled his pledge to open the club up to the fans, thousands of whom became shareholders. The funds generated and subsequent prudent financial management have helped transform Celtic as a competitive force and commercial operation.

Not everything has, or could have, met with general approval but few would dispute that the club is in a far healthier state today than it was four years ago. The awesome new stadium that has sprung up far quicker than anyone could have hoped is testament to that fact. The new Celtic Park stands as an imposing monument to the vision, dedication and courage of the man who laid his reputation and money on the line and those who had the faith to back him.

Fergus McCann, while not everyone's cup of tea, with his direct, assertive style, and apparent disregard at times for media opinion, has undoubtedly delivered. The stadium is in place. A club that had become a laughing stock has had its credibility restored. And the team has, amidst the bloodletting, been transformed and returned to winning ways.

It now only remains to see how he intends to redeem that final pledge to ensure that the club is left in appropriate hands.

The Burns 'Bhoy'

Tommy Burns was a hugely popular choice to replace Macari in the 'close-season' of 1994. The fans knew that, as well as blossoming tactical and managerial skills, he would bring a deep and genuine passion for the club he had served with such distinction as a player. The fact that his Kilmarnock assistant and fellow 'Old Bhoy', Billy Stark, with whom he was developing such a promising partnership, was part of the package, was a bonus.

Their three-year tenure would be characterised by free-flowing, attacking football in the traditional Celtic mould, particularly in the middle season of 1995/96, when they really ought to have won the Championship. Yet, despite losing only one game and producing, at times, the most imaginative and exciting football of any Celtic side since the days of the 'Lisbon Lions', exemplified by the 5-0 annihilation of Aberdeen on 1st April, 1966, their efforts came to nothing.

Burns' first season brought agony and ecstasy in almost equal measures. It seemed as if he would end the trophy famine stretching back to the Scottish Cup of 1989 at the very first attempt, when the final of the League Cup was reached in opposition to first-division Raith Rovers. It was to be total heartbreak for Celtic, though, as the cup was snatched from their grasp in a nightmare Ibrox shoot-out. The unfortunate Paul McStay, it was, who missed the vital kick on a day that must rank as one of the club's all-time lows.

That Burns and his squad rallied so well from such a crushing experience is to their eternal credit. Before the season was out, they had battled their way to the Scottish Cup Final of 1995. The burden of expectation was, inevitably, even greater than in the League Cup and it was not eased in the run-in by a media that was a little too eager to highlight the fact that Celtic again faced dangerous First Division opposition in Airdrie.

Scottish Cup Final, 1995

Hampden on 27th May, 1995 was never going to be easy for Celtic, despite the boost of a tremendous 3-0 'home' Premier League win over Rangers just a few weeks previously. Hampden, of course, was Celtic's 'home' that season due to reconstruction work at Celtic Park – but it was never a very comfortable home, which, if anything, was a disadvantage on the day.

It was never likely to be a memorable final, given the tensions involved and Airdrie were just the sort of gritty opponents who would make life very difficult, indeed, given the slightest encouragement. The result was really all that mattered, as another reverse would have spelt total disaster for Celtic – and Tommy Burns.

As it was, the desired early lead was gained, courtesy of a majestic Pierre van Hooijdonk header from an inch-perfect Tosh McKinlay cross on the nine-minute mark. The release of tension was manifested in a tremendous terracing eruption. Surely, now, Celtic would relax and go on to win comfortably. Only, it didn't quite work out like that and the remaining eighty minutes or so did nothing for the frayed nerves of Celtic fans in the ground and watching screens all across the country.

When the dust (and the nerves) had settled, though, the old trophy was decked in green and white ribbons again, at last and the happiest summer for years was in prospect, particularly, perhaps, for the Cup Final line-up:

Bonner: Boyd, McKinlay, Vata, McNally, Grant, McLaughlin, McStay, van Hooijdonk, Donnelly & Collins.

While that day was a potential platform to build on, it proved to be the only honour Tommy Burns would bring to Celtic. It might have been very different had things worked out better at crucial stages of the following two seasons. A plague of draws and a distinct tendency to get caught on the break, though, cost Burns' cavalier sides dearly, particularly against Rangers – a fatal flaw!

Throughout his spell in charge, Tommy had an uneasy relationship with Fergus McCann. More than once, Tommy's frustrations boiled over into public outbursts that undoubtedly put him under even greater pressure. But he was a passionate man who burned with the desire to restore Celtic to their rightful place and could not bear to see that aim thwarted, as he saw it, in any way.

He paid the ultimate price towards the end of season 1996/97, leaving behind some golden memories of not only that crucial Scottish Cup breakthrough but also the wonderful play of gifted players like Pierre van Hooijdonk, Andy Thom, Jorge Cadete, Paolo di Canio, Alan Stubbs and others he brought to the club, some of whom, sadly, left in controversial circumstances.

Wim Who?

After much 'close-season' speculation as to who would succeed Tommy Burns, controversial football general manager, Jock Brown, finally unveiled Wim Jansen and revealed that he had always been the target. The media and more importantly, the fans, who had become increasingly restive at the onset of the new season without a head coach in place, were not entirely convinced.

However, as usual, they were prepared to give Jansen the benefit of the doubt and let him get on with the job. He certainly had an impressive playing pedigree, with two World Cup Final appearances for Holland and two European finals with Feyenoord (including *that* one) to his credit.

When the action got underway, the omens were far from good. The first two league games brought demoralising defeats from Hibs and Dunfermline Athletic. Alarm bells were sounding and early doubts set in about the wisdom of this appointment of Celtic's first foreign coach.

The league form settled after that, though, and the steady climb from bottom back to top was soon underway. Jansen's side began to play a much more studied style of football than his predecessor's, built on solidity at the back, good possession and fast, incisive forward movement. It was worlds away from the Burns method and not to everyone's liking, by any means. Undoubtedly effective, though, and enough to see them through to the first final of the year, at Ibrox.

League Cup Final, 1997

CELTIC's supremacy on this occasion completely washed away former huge disappointment in the competition and gave genuine cause for future optimism. The flowing performance, with *'Man of the Match'*, Morten Wieghorst, immense in midfield and awesome in his forward thrusting runs, was a joy to behold. The normally dangerous opposition of Dundee United was virtually nullified as Celtic strode confidently to victory.

Towering Marc Rieper set the ball rolling in twenty-one minutes with a header, steered in off the post, reminiscent of his great predecessor, Billy McNeill's early strike in the 1969 Scottish Cup Final. Two minutes later, the 'Bhoys' were on 'Easy Street', as Henrik Larsson fastened onto a loose ball to strike a shot from just outside the box. Maurice Malpas' attemped block simply sent the ball looping over his helpless goalkeeper, Sieb Dykstra, into the United net.

It was all over bar the shouting. Even with well over an hour left to play, the destination of the cup was well and truly fixed. On fifty-nine minutes, Craig Burley set the seal on a commanding performance with a close-range diving header to convert Regi Blinker's withering cross for 3-0.

It could have been more emphatic, as Blinker and Andy Thom (twice) had great chances to increase the margin of victory–but it didn't really matter. There had been more than enough to savour for one day as it was.

In the explosive celebratory aftermath, as acclamation rolled around Ibrox and waves of rapturous joy cascaded from the stands, Wim Jansen appeared overcome – mystified, almost, by the intensity of it all. If this was the reaction to the *least* of the major trophies, what could he expect in the event of a Championship?

Time would tell . . . in more ways than one, as it happens.

The convincingly victorious Celtic line-up was:

Gould: Boyd, Mahe, McNamara (Annoni), Rieper, Stubbs, Larsson, Burley, Thom (Donnelly), Wieghorst, Blinker (Lambert).

So far, so good. This Jansen was clearly onto something. The real test lay ahead, though. Nine seasons had elapsed since the last Celtic League Championship – and Rangers had won the title every year! It had been sheer agony watching Jock Stein's great 'Nine-in-a-Row' being equalled the previous year. The prospect of it being surpassed was anathema. Could this little Dutchman prevent it?

Joyously, the answer was 'yes' but it was all a bit of a struggle, even after the euphoric 2-0 New Year 'Old Firm' victory, featuring those marvellous goals from Craig Burley and Paul Lambert.

Still, the manner of the League Championship success of 1997/98 was of less importance than its significance. The rot had been stopped, the unthinkable avoided and Celtic were back on top. The explosion of relief and ecstasy that greeted Harald Brattbakk's swoop for the second and clinching goal against St Johnstone on the last day of the season, proclaimed Celtic 'Champions' at last and Wim Jansen a Celtic 'instant legend'.

Three days after leading Celtic to the Championship, Wim Jansen had resigned. Jansen and the Club had agreed that if he or the Club did not wish to continue after one year, neither party would comment until July, or when a replacement had been identified. In March 1998 though, Jansen made it public that a break clause existed. In the period until the end of the season, Celtic won only three of their remaining eight matches.

Wim Jansen's resignation, although not perhaps unexpected by some, and Murdo MacLeod's subsequent dismissal, removed much of the joy and left fans stunned, hurt, and facing another summer of uncertainty.

Dr Venglos

The media frenzy to uncover and reveal Jansen's successor reached new heights before, during and after the World Cup Finals, in France but didn't even come close to the eventual truth.

Dr Jozef Venglos was introduced to the world as Celtic head coach on Friday 17th July, 1998. Following the pre-season tour to Holland, he took up the reins for the preliminary tie against St Patrick's Athletic that preceded the final qualifier v Croatia Zagreb for a place in the 1998/99 Champions' League.

The future health of Celtic now rests in the Doctor's hands.

Appendix 1: Celtic Social Mission Statement

CELTIC FOOTBALL CLUB is legendary and as with most legends, as much myth as fact surrounds its history and what the club stands for today. The *Social Mission Statement* aims to simply define what the club stands for and seeks to promote within society.

History

Celtic Football Club was founded in 1888. Its principal founder was a Marist Brother named Walfrid. The club had two principal aims:

The first aim was to raise funds to provide food for the poor of the East End of Glasgow, an area of the city that was greatly impoverished and had a very high rate of infant mortality.

Within the East End was a large Irish community and friction was growing between the native Glaswegians and the new influx of Irish. Brother Walfrid saw the need for social integration and his vision was a football club that Scottish and Irish, Protestants and Catholics alike could support. A new football club would be a vehicle to bring the communities together and this was the second aim. The Marist Brother sought for the club to have both a Scottish and Irish identity and hence the club's name, 'Celtic', came about, representing a bridge of cultures across the Irish Sea.

Current Positioning of Celtic Football Club

Celtic Football Club is a Scottish football club with proud Irish links. The primary business of Celtic is as a football club. It is run on a professional business basis with no political agenda. However, the club has a wider role and the responsibility of being a major Scottish social institution promoting health, wellbeing and social integration.

Who is Celtic Football Club for?

Celtic Football Club is for people who want to support a football club that strives for excellence in Scotland and Europe, is proud of its history, supportive of its local community and seeks to support the following aims:-

"To maximise all opportunities to disassociate the club from sectarianism and bigotry of any kind. To promote Celtic as a club for all people, regardless of sex, age, religion, race or ability."

Summary

Celtic is a club for everyone who believes in football as a medium for healthy pleasure, entertainment and social integration. The club has been and always will simply aim to be the team of the people.

Reproduced from the *Celtic Directory of Services*
by kind permission of Celtic Football Club.

Appendix 2: The Celtic Honours

'Specials'

Glasgow Exhibition Cup (1902)

Scottish League Commemorative Shield (1904/05 – 1909/10)

Empire Exhibition Trophy (1938)

Victory in Europe Cup (1945)

St Mungo Cup (1951)

Coronation Cup (1953)

European Champions' Cup (1967)

League Championships (36)

1892/93, 1893/94, 1895/96, 1897/98, 1904/05,
1905/06, 1906/07, 1907/08, 1908/09, 1909/10,
1913/14, 1914/15, 1915/16, 1916/17, 1918/19,
1921/22, 1925/26, 1935/36, 1937/38, 1953/54,
1965/66, 1966/67, 1967/68, 1968/69, 1969/70,
1970/71, 1971/72, 1972/73, 1973/74, 1976/77,
1978/79, 1980/81, 1981/82, 1985/86, 1987/88,
1997/98.

Scottish Cups (30)

1892, 1899, 1900, 1904, 1907, 1908,
1911, 1912, 1914, 1923, 1925, 1927,
1931, 1933, 1937, 1951, 1954, 1965,
1967, 1969, 1971, 1972, 1974, 1975,
1977, 1980, 1985, 1988, 1989, 1995.

Scottish League Cups (10) 1956, 1957, 1965, 1966, 1967, 1968, 1969, 1974, 1982, 1997.

Glasgow Cups (29)

1890/91, 1891/92, 1894/95, 1895/96, 1904/05,
1905/06, 1906/07, 1907/08, 1909/10, 1915/16,
1916/17, 1919/20, 1920/21, 1926/27, 1927/28,
1928/29, 1930/31, 1938/39, 1940/41, 1948/49,
1955/56, 1961/62, 1963/64, 1964/65, 1966/67,
1967/68, 1969/70, 1974/75 (Shared with Rangers
after a 2-2 draw), 1981/82.

Glasgow Charity Cups (28)

1891/92, 1892/93, 1893/94, 1894/95,
1895/96, 1898/99, 1902/03, 1904/05,
1907/08, 1911/12, 1912/13, 1913/14,
1914/15, 1915/16, 1916/17, 1917/18,
1919/20, 1920/21, 1923/24, 1925/26,
1935/36, 1936/37, 1937/38, 1942/43,
1949/50, 1952/53, 1958/59, 1960/61
(Shared with Clyde after a 1-1 draw).

Appendix 3: Managerial Records

COUNTING the six categories of *Appendix 2* as the principal competitions in which Celtic have competed over the past 110 years, the club has amassed a total of 140 major honours (36 League Championships, 30 Scottish Cups, 10 League Cups, 29 Glasgow Cups, 28 Charity Cups and 7 'Specials').

The Managers
William Maley 1888 - 1940
Jimmy McStay 1940 - 1945
Jimmy McGrory 1945 - 1965
Jock Stein 1965 - 1978
Billy McNeill 1978 - 1983 & 1987 - 1991
David Hay 1983 - 1987
Liam Brady 1991 - 1993
Lou Macari 1993 - 1994
Tommy Burns 1994 - 1997
Wim Jansen 1997 - 1998

The attribution of the above honours to the ten managers (excluding 'caretaker' spells, such as Sean Fallon's deputising for Jock Stein during the 1975/76 season and treating William Maley as effective manager in the years before his official appointment) is as follows:

Manager	League	Cup	L'ge Cup	Gl'w Cup	Ch. Cup	'Specials.'	Total
Maley	19	15	0	18	23	3	78
McStay	0	0	0	1	1	1	3
McGrory	1	2	2	5	4	2	16
Stein	10	8	6	4	0	1	29
McNeill	4	3	1	1	0	0	9
Hay	1	1	0	0	0	0	2
Brady	0	0	0	0	0	0	0
Macari	0	0	0	0	0	0	0
Burns	0	1	0	0	0	0	1
Jansen	1	0	1	0	0	0	2
Totals	36	30	10	29	28	7	140

In pure statistical terms, then, Willie Maley, whose 78 honours represent some 56% of the club's total haul of 'major' silverware, has to be rated the most successful Celtic manager of them all. Of course, bare statistics never tell the whole story and most modern commentators would probably consider the Stein era, when 'The Big Man' amassed 25 major trophies in just twelve active seasons, as the true 'Golden Age', to date, of *The Celtic Football Club.*

Understandably, the most impressive back-to-back winning streaks happened under Maley and Stein, whose collective contribution of major trophies equates to an astonishing 76% of the club's 110-year total. Maley bagged 6 consecutive League Championships from 1904/05-1909/10, specially commemorated by the magnificent Scottish League Shield, 4 Glasgow Cups on the trot between 1904/05 and 1907/08 and (in two bursts) the Charity Cup, first 5 times in a row, from 1891/92-1895/96, then 7 times, from 1911/12-1917/18. Big Jock, of course, really hit the jackpot with his 'Nine-in-a-Row' League Championship run from 1965/66-1973/74, as well as ringing up 5 League Cups in succession from 1965-1969.

Other memorable managerial milestones include the historic 'Specials' : Maley's trio, the Glasgow and Empire Exhibition Trophies and the League Shield; McStay's Victory in Europe Cup; McGrory's St Mungo and Coronation Cups and the daddy of them all, Stein's European Cup. Billy McNeill's 'Centenary Double' was a fitting and unforgettable highlight and for sheer breathtaking excitement, it would be hard to beat the last-day 1985/86 title thriller at Love Street under Davie Hay. That classic brought echoes of a similar feat in the 4-2 Championship-clinching demolition of Rangers at Celtic Park on the final day of McNeill's first season in charge (1978/79). And of course, we must never forget Wim Jansen's priceless contribution towards ensuring that the heartbreak of Stein's magnificent league record being surpassed did not have to be endured last season.

Good luck to Jozef Venglos – he has some hard acts to follow.